W9-DJJ-761

ASHE Higher Education Report: Volume 33, Number 3
Kelly Ward, Lisa E. Wolf-Wendel, Series Editors

Economically and Educationally Challenged Students in Higher Education: Access to Outcomes

MaryBeth Walpole

Economically and Educationally Challenged Students in Higher Education:
Access to Outcomes
MaryBeth Walpole
ASHE Higher Education Report: Volume 33, Number 3
Kelly Ward, Lisa E. Wolf-Wendel, Series Editors

ISSN 1551-6970   electronic ISSN 1554-6306   ISBN 978-0-4702-2535-6

The ASHE Higher Education Report is part of the Jossey-Bass Higher and Adult
Education Series and is published six times a year by Wiley Subscription Services,
Inc., A Wiley Company, at Jossey-Bass, 989 Market Street, San Francisco,
California 94103-1741.

For subscription information, see the Back Issue/Subscription Order Form
in the back of this volume.

CALL FOR PROPOSALS: Prospective authors are strongly encouraged to contact
Kelly Ward (kaward@wsu.edu) or Lisa Wolf-Wendel (lwolf@ku.edu). See "About
the ASHE Higher Education Report Series" in the back of this volume.

Visit the Jossey-Bass Web site at **www.josseybass.com.**

Printed in the United States of America on acid-free recycled paper.

The ASHE Higher Education Report is indexed in CIJE: Current Index to Jour-
nals in Education (ERIC), Current Abstracts (EBSCO), Education Index/Abstracts
(H.W. Wilson), ERIC Database (Education Resources Information Center),
Higher Education Abstracts (Claremont Graduate University), IBR & IBZ: Inter-
national Bibliographies of Periodical Literature (K.G. Saur), Resources in Education
(ERIC).

Advisory Board

BICENTENNIAL
BICENTENNIAL
1807
WILEY
2007
BICENTENNIAL
BICENTENNIAL

THE WILEY BICENTENNIAL—KNOWLEDGE FOR GENERATIONS

*E*ach generation has its unique needs and aspirations. When Charles Wiley first opened his small printing shop in lower Manhattan in 1807, it was a generation of boundless potential searching for an identity. And we were there, helping to define a new American literary tradition. Over half a century later, in the midst of the Second Industrial Revolution, it was a generation focused on building the future. Once again, we were there, supplying the critical scientific, technical, and engineering knowledge that helped frame the world. Throughout the 20th Century, and into the new millennium, nations began to reach out beyond their own borders and a new international community was born. Wiley was there, expanding its operations around the world to enable a global exchange of ideas, opinions, and know-how.

For 200 years, Wiley has been an integral part of each generation's journey, enabling the flow of information and understanding necessary to meet their needs and fulfill their aspirations. Today, bold new technologies are changing the way we live and learn. Wiley will be there, providing you the must-have knowledge you need to imagine new worlds, new possibilities, and new opportunities.

Generations come and go, but you can always count on Wiley to provide you the knowledge you need, when and where you need it!

WILLIAM J. PESCE
PRESIDENT AND CHIEF EXECUTIVE OFFICER

PETER BOOTH WILEY
CHAIRMAN OF THE BOARD

Contents

Executive Summary

Low socioeconomic (SES) college students' college attendance rate is 30 percent lower than their more advantaged peers, a gap that has been consistent for decades. These students face unique challenges in every aspect of postsecondary education, and yet despite this knowledge and significant amounts of research, little progress has been made in closing the gap. In this volume, I highlight the issues surrounding low-SES, low-income, working-class, and first-generation students' access to, enrollment and experiences in, and outcomes of higher education.

In studying these groups of students, researchers typically focus on one group—either low SES, low income, working class, or first generation—without referencing work with other groups. They also typically focus on one part of the educational pipeline, for example, college access or graduate school attendance, rather than exploring students' process and progress holistically. These practices have resulted in de facto research silos. This volume incorporates research on each of these groups of students and includes research on college access, experiences in college, and outcomes of college. Following a review of how scholars define socioeconomic status and its component variables and how those definitions are operationalized in higher education research, I suggest using the term *economically and educationally challenged* (EEC) students. This umbrella term encompasses low-SES, low-income, working-class, and first-generation students and may provide researchers with a means of dismantling the de facto silos and connecting the research, with the hope that such connections will yield new and important insights to reduce the 30 percent gap in attendance.

Following a focus on definitions used in research, I discuss the conceptual frameworks and models that flow from scholars' definitions and operationalizations of social class: status attainment theory, human capital theory, the financial nexus model, Bourdieuian theory, and critical race theory. Connections between these theories exist, and several researchers have included elements of multiple frameworks in their own conceptualizations and models. Increasing the complexity of theoretical frameworks and models is needed to understand and explain the complexity of EEC students' lives and decisions.

Knowing and understanding the definitions used and the conceptual frameworks employed in research on EEC students provides a foundation for then examining students' access to, experiences in, and outcomes of college attendance. Much of the research has focused on college access, and EEC students are at a disadvantage because they do not have sufficient access to rigorous course work in high school and lack necessary information about applying to and attending college. These students typically attend less selective rather than highly selective institutions when they do enroll. Very little research has focused on EEC students' academic and cocurricular experiences in college, but the evidence indicates that they work more, study less, and are less involved than their non-EEC peers while attending college and are less likely to persist and graduate. They are also less likely to attend graduate school. More research is needed to explore differences in cognitive gains and aspirations during the undergraduate years and in income following college.

Students often have multiple social locations and identities in addition to their social class locations that affect their postsecondary process. The research in this area is relatively new and underdeveloped and has also focused disproportionately on college access. All EEC students, regardless of gender, race, or ethnicity, face challenges in accessing, persisting, and graduating from college. The intersections of these identity statuses and educational processes and outcomes are nonlinear and deserve additional exploration.

EEC students attend different types of institutions from their peers, and many scholars believe that different types of institutions promote differential outcomes for low-SES students. However, other scholars have shown that the type of institution does not matter once incoming characteristics are controlled. Many institutions enrolling EEC students have responded with specific policies and programs for EEC students. Programs such as summer transition programs and additional in-semester assistance provide much needed assistance to students and can help increase retention rates.

There is much work to be done in this area to improve the attendance, persistence, and graduation rates of EEC students. There is still much intellectual territory for scholars to explore, especially regarding EEC students' academic and cocurricular experiences and their outcomes. The intellectual territory is particularly open to researchers who are interested in multiple identities or those who are focused on the synergy between particular types of institutions and EEC students. Policymakers also have a significant opportunity to contribute. First, the importance of access to academically rigorous courses for EEC students is difficult to overstate, yet these students' access continues to be restricted. Policymakers can also focus their attention on financial aid policy because EEC students' progress is contingent on finding ways to increase aid. Practitioners also have a role in assisting these students.

Social class in our society is often hidden or disguised, and EEC students may be difficult to recognize on campuses. Practitioners need to find ways to reach out to these students, understand the challenges these students face, and find ways to assist them in their quest for a college education. Researchers and policymakers have a responsibility to look for ways to provide information to practitioners so that they may act on it; practitioners also have a responsibility to seek such information. Only by fostering communication across domains can EEC students' concerns be addressed holistically.

Foreword

American colleges and universities are well known internationally for providing access and opportunity to students of varying levels of ability, educational and family backgrounds, and economic status. In spite of such access, there is a wide and persistent gap in the college going rates of low and high socioeconomic high school graduates. Access to college does not automatically translate to enrollment in and success with the college going experience.

MaryBeth Walpole's monograph *Economically and Educationally Challenged Students in Higher Education: Access to Outcomes* provides important theoretical, conceptual, and empirical insight to help tease out some of the issues that surround opportunity gaps that exist in higher education. Walpole admirably takes on the tall task of defining the nuances of social class and how it affects students in their collegiate experience and associated outcomes. Walpole calls for a holistic view of students by offering the umbrella term of "economically and educationally challenged students" as a way to think more broadly about four definitional categories-socioeconomic status, parental income, parent education, and parent occupation. These categories are often used and studied interchangeably, but relying on a thorough review of the literature, Walpole clearly illustrates the challenges associated with clumping students together without definition and delineation of terms and categories.

Researchers and practitioners interested in access and outcomes of economically and educationally challenged students will find Walpole's work to be helpful in how they think about students' background and to also more fully understand the nuances of issues associated with social class. It's easy to think of social class solely in economic terms and it's also easy to forget that these same terms in turn shape educational and personal choices. This monograph teases out the different terminologies and constructs associated with social class to provide readers with deeper understanding of how terminologies are used in research and practice. Walpole's work is by far one of the most helpful in terms of clearly defining concepts associated with social class such as socioeconomic status, parental income, parental educational background, and parental occupation. All of these constructs are well known to contribute to social class but how and in what ways is the focus of this book. These terms tend to be bantered about in research and practice with the assumption that readers and users are agreement with the definitions of these terms when in fact a thorough analysis of research in the area reveals a fair amount of what Walpole calls "definitional disunity."

Throughout the monograph, Walpole defines terms, defines variables, and gives examples of how particular constructs related to social class are used in research. Walpole does an admirable job of deconstructing research constructs in the field and shows how they are used to contribute to particular findings. Researchers interested in economically and educationally challenged student concerns as well as those just starting in the field will find the monograph to be particularly helpful.

The primary purpose of the ASHE Monograph Series is to synthesize and analyze literature on a given topic. Walpole's monograph does a particularly good job of presenting the literature, analyzing it, and situating the findings in larger research and policy contexts. This is particularly important with research on college students related to social class because so many related concepts go undefined. Definitions of words like "first generation college student" are assumed to be common knowledge. Walpole points out the problem with such assumptions by examining related research and findings. Looking at research related to social class holistically as Walpole does in this monograph, points to the importance of moving beyond silo thinking when it comes to social class and college students. If a student is first generation, African American, and from a low socioeconomic background then these aspects of a student do not exist in isolation of one another. Too often, however, research on these particular aspects of a student is done without full consideration of interrelatedness of a student's background.

While not all students who are economically challenged are educationally challenged, existing research shows that collectively students that fall into both categories can face similar obstacles to access and challenges associated with involvement while in college. An umbrella term (economically and educationally challenged) provides a way for researchers to think differently about their work, provides a mechanism for researchers to learn from one another's work, and can help push forward collective thinking about research related to social class.

The opportunity gap in higher education has been persistent and the umbrella term that Walpole calls for offers a new way of thinking as a means to provide insight for research, policy, and practice. The umbrella term may also be helpful to create political mobilization for it pulls together groups with similar experiences and who face similar obstacles in higher education. Thinking holistically about similar groups is a way to acknowledge the structural issues that economically and educationally disadvantaged students face in their experience with higher education. A holistic view also provides a new and different way to think about individual agency. Without an approach to research and practice that simultaneously acknowledges structure and agency the opportunity gap will persist and given the knowledge and resources in higher education related to social class it is time for the gap to be addressed and narrowed.

Kelly Ward
Series Editor

Published online in Wiley InterScience
(www.interscience.wiley.com) • DOI: 10.1002/aehe.3303

Introduction

A 30 PERCENT GAP EXISTS BETWEEN THE COLLEGE-GOING rates of low- and high-socioeconomic-status (SES) high school graduates (Bedsworth, Colby, and Doctor, 2006), a gap that has not diminished in decades (Gladieux and Swail, 1998; McPherson and Schapiro, 1991). This gap is disturbing, and its longevity is even more distressing. Clearly scholars, practitioners, and policymakers must work together to reduce and eliminate this opportunity gap. Although low-income students have been enrolled in American colleges and universities since their inception, the numbers of such students were initially small, and they quickly became the minority (Allmendinger, 1975; Wechsler, 1997). Their minority status has continued unabated, and garnered significant attention from policymakers and scholars (Astin and Oseguera, 2004; Bowen, Kurzweil, and Tobin, 2005; Hearn, 1984, 1990, 1991; Karabel, 2005; Karabel and Astin, 1975; Karen, 1991; McDonough, 1997; Perna and Titus, 2004), but it has not been reduced (Gladieux and Swail, 1998; McPherson and Schapiro, 1991).

Expanding access to higher education has been recommended by governmental commissions and reports since the 1940s (Freeland, 1997) and federally supported since the institution of the GI Bill in the 1940s and need-based aid in the 1950s (McPherson and Schapiro, 1991). Although overall college-going rates have expanded tremendously since the 1940s and 1950s, low-SES students are still underrepresented in colleges and universities (Bedsworth et al., 2006). Most recently, access to college for low-SES students and students from racial and ethnic minority groups has been one focus of the Spellings Commission report (U.S. Department of Education, 2006).

Despite this consistent attention over several decades, the Spellings report drew new interest to the fact that students from families of modest means and modest educational backgrounds are challenged significantly in gaining access to and graduating from colleges and universities, especially four-year institutions and more selective colleges. In fact, only a third of low-SES youth enroll in college, and less than 15 percent earn a four-year degree (Bedsworth et al., 2006). According to the most recent studies, students who come from low-income families and whose parents did not attend college are less likely to enroll in college, enroll in a four-year institution, and persist regardless of ability than are their higher-income peers who are not the first in their families to go to college (Astin, 1993; Astin and Oseguera, 2004; Bedsworth et al., 2006; Cabrera, Burkhum, and La Nasa, 2005; Hearn, 1984, 1990, 1991; Karabel and Astin, 1975; Karen, 1991; McDonough, 1997; Pascarella and Terenzini, 1991, 2005; Perna and Titus, 2004; Terenzini, Cabrera, and Bernal, 2001; Tinto, 2006; Titus, 2006a, 2006c).

These students' access to and success in higher education are important because completing college and obtaining a bachelor's degree is seen as a critical component of social mobility (Bedsworth et al., 2006; Bowen et al., 2005; Hossler, Schmit, and Vesper, 1999; Karabel, 2005; Karabel and Astin, 1975; Pascarella and Terenzini, 1991; Tinto, 2006). However, obtaining a bachelor's degree is an achievement built on previous educational attainment and experiences and is also dependent on aspirations and persistence. Differences have been found in students' attainment, experiences, aspirations, and persistence based on their SES, on whether their parents attended or graduated from college, and on their social class.

As a group, students from low socioeconomic backgrounds, students whose parents did not attend or graduate from college, and students whose parents work at lower-status jobs or have lower incomes have lower educational aspirations, persistence rates, and educational attainment than do their peers from high-SES backgrounds (Astin, 1993; Astin and Oseguera, 2004; Bedsworth et al., 2006; Cabrera et al., 2005; Hearn, 1984, 1990, 1991; Karabel, 2005; Karabel and Astin, 1975; Karen, 1991; McDonough, 1997; Pascarella and Terenzini, 1991, 2005; Perna and Titus, 2004; Terenzini et al., 2001; Tinto, 2006; Titus, 2006a, 2006c). The differences begin at a young age, are cumulative, and result from many forces.

Although most scholars, policymakers, and practitioners are aware of the effects that SES, income, or social class have on students' educational experiences and attainment, social class in the U.S. context is notoriously difficult to define. One reason is the demographic diversity, which conflates social class with race and ethnicity (Hacker, 1995). Another reason is that our myth of the American dream attributes success to individual effort, minimizing any structural contributions (McNamee and Miller, 2004). Finally, there is a lack of recognition of one's social class status in relationship to the majority of the country. Most Americans can look at the people around them on a daily basis and see those who are both worse off and better off economically, leading to a widespread belief among Americans that they are middle class.

When scholars discuss the general concept of social class, it involves educational attainment, occupational status, and income, but also tends to expand discrete notions of economic and educational capital by including values, lifestyles, and ideology, which work in concert to shape an individual's worldview (Bourdieu, 1990; Cookson and Persell, 1985; Domhoff, 1983; Gilbert and Kahl, 1993; Kohn, 1977; Persell and Cookson, 1990). *Working class* and *upper class* are terms researchers use to describe specific sections of the class structure, as well as class-specific lifestyles, attitudes, beliefs, and values—in other words, class cultures (Domhoff, 1983; Gilbert and Kahl, 1993; Kohn, 1977; Persell and Cookson, 1990). It is important to note that these class cultures result from rather than cause economic and educational differences (McNamee and Miller, 2004). In defining social class and SES, many studies use relative definitions based on the sample, resulting in a range of definitions. Although these relative definitions are appropriate for research and supported by Jencks and colleagues (1972, 1994), because a person's SES is relative and contextual, the diversity in definitions makes cross-study comparison, analysis, and synthesis arduous.

Moreover, significant overlap and a certain amount of ambiguity exist in these definitions and the ways they are operationalized in research, in part because as a society, we have many terms to describe social class. While working-class people are usually on the low end of the socioeconomic continuum, the term *low SES* can include additional groups, such as unemployed poor people and a group often termed the working poor. The same is true of the high socioeconomic strata, which can include upper-middle or upper-class people, as well as people with high incomes. Class status in the United States consists of a continuum based on criteria such as income, educational attainment, lifestyle, values, and beliefs, as well as how people perceive similarities and differences among groups (Jackman and Jackman, 1983), adding to the difficulty in defining, describing, and studying particular social class locations.

In addition, in the United States, *social class* is a relative term; Americans generally define themselves as middle class because they typically know people who are both better off and worse off economically or more or less well educated. Furthermore, social class can be disguised, and people sometimes deliberately attempt to conceal their social class because they are ashamed or want to conform to the social class norms that surround them. Thus, social class in the U.S. context is complex, with overlapping layers that can be examined and defined in different ways, making research and comparisons difficult (McNamee and Miller, 2004). However, an understanding of social class and how it affects educational experiences and outcomes is critical to improving those experiences and outcomes and is the focus here.

Such an understanding is particularly important to higher education scholars, researchers, and practitioners because a college education is a crucial component of our nation's opportunity structure (Bowen et al., 2005; Karabel, 2005; Karen, 1991). In order to ensure the integrity of that structure for all students, and particularly those who face challenges due to their social class backgrounds, it is critical to first understand how researchers, policymakers, and practitioners define these students in research and then to understand how their access to college, their academic and cocurricular experiences in college, and their educational and career outcomes after college are affected by those definitions. In studies of college access, college student persistence, and college outcomes, scholars often focus on one attribute or variable, such as income, parental educational status, parental occupation, or some combination to form socioeconomic status (Terenzini et al., 2001; Tinto, 2006). This volume examines and integrates literature on how social class, socioeconomic status, parental income, and first-generation status affect educational achievement and attainment on the postsecondary level. This holistic view will assist researchers, practitioners, and policymakers as they seek to assist this underrepresented population of students.

Organization

After this introduction, I focus on how scholars define *socioeconomic status* and its component variables and how those definitions are operationalized in higher education research. These definitions fall into four overlapping categories, and I suggest a new umbrella term and provide reasons why such a term may be appropriate. The volume then examines conceptual frameworks and models that flow from scholars' definitions and operationalizations of social class: status attainment theory, human capital theory, the financial nexus model, Bourdieuian theory, and critical race theory. These have been used most frequently to explore and explain inequitable access to, experiences in, and outcomes of higher education.

This material then provides a foundation for examining students' access to, experiences in, and outcomes of college attendance. I have, when possible, grouped studies together by the four definitional categories in order to highlight the similarity in students' experiences and outcomes between definitional groupings. I have also, where appropriate, highlighted use of the theoretical frameworks I discuss.

Since students often have multiple social locations that affect their educational process, I next look at students' multiple identities, including examining the synergistic effects of being from a particular social class location while also belonging to specific racial and ethnic groups. I also explore how gender intersects with social class and racial/ethnic identities to shape college access, experiences, and outcomes. Because students' actions are made within an institutional context, the volume then turns to the contributions of organizational responses and policies specific to this group of students. Finally, the volume concludes with implications and recommendations for researchers, practitioners, and policymakers. In order to draw those conclusions on how to increase the numbers of low-SES students who attend and graduate from colleges and universities, it is critical to first understand how researchers, policymakers, and practitioners define these students.

Definitions

IN ORDER TO EXAMINE AND IMPROVE LOW-SES STUDENTS' access to, experiences in, and outcomes of college, we must first define these students. This may seem relatively straightforward, but in the higher education research it is quite complex. Although researchers agree that students from families with low incomes, whose parents did not attend college, or whose parents work at lower-status occupations are less likely to attend or graduate from college (Astin, 1993; Astin and Oseguera, 2004; Bedsworth et al., 2006; Cabrera et al., 2005; Hearn, 1984, 1990, 1991; Karabel, 2005; Karabel and Astin, 1975; Karen, 1991; McDonough, 1997; Pascarella and Terenzini, 1991, 2005; Perna and Titus, 2004; Terenzini et al., 2001; Tinto, 2006; Titus, 2006a, 2006c), there has been little cohesiveness in defining and examining these students' experiences. Some researchers rely solely on family income (Akerhielm, Berger, Hooker, and Wise, 1998; Paulsen and St. John, 2002; Perna, 2005; Teranishi, Ceja, Antonio, Allen, and McDonough, 2004); others believe that parental education is the key (Choy, Horn, Nunez, and Chen, 2000; Ishitani, 2006; Nunez and Cuccaro-Alamin, 1998; Pascarella, Pierson, Wolniak, and Terenzini, 2004; Rodriguez, 2003; Terenzini, Springer, Yaeger, Pascarella, and Nora, 1996); and still others insist on using parental occupation to investigate this population (Casey, 2005; Goldstein, 1974; Littrell, 1999; Luzzo, 1992; O'Dair, 2003; Tett, 2004). Many believe a combination of these three, along with items in the home such as computers or books, define socioeconomic status (Carnevale and Rose, 2004; Perna and Titus, 2004; Terenzini et al., 2001; Titus, 2006c; Walpole, 2003; Williams, Leppel, and Waldauer, 2005).

Moreover, some researchers focus on first-generation students in higher education without a clear link to income or SES (Choy et al., 2000; Ishitani, 2006; Nunez and Cuccaro-Alamin, 1998; Pascarella et al., 2004; Rodriguez, 2003; Terenzini et al., 1996). And while SES has been acknowledged as a significant variable within higher education research, it is more often controlled for than investigated as a variable whose effects are important to understand (Paulsen and St. John, 2002). This lack of investigations based on SES and lack of definitional consistency have hampered a holistic appreciation of the roles of parental education, occupation, income, or SES in higher education research. We will review the differing definitions with respect to higher education and the ramifications of this definitional disunity.

Historical Development of Current Categories

Karl Marx (1956) defined social class in economic terms, determined by an individual's relationship to the means of production. Max Weber (1946) disagreed with what he viewed as Marx's dichotomous owner/nonowner notion of classes and instead identified and defined status groups as connected and overlapping classes, expanding Marx's economic definition to include patterns of consumption and lifestyles. Weber saw these groups as communities with concrete signals of membership eligibility, such as location of residence, family history, and choice of marriage partner.

For Weber (1946), stratification of status groups occurs as groups attempt to, and succeed in, monopolizing certain material goods, such as a college education, that form the basis for exclusivity. As will become clear, many of our current concepts related to socioeconomic status and social class are rooted in the work of these early authors. Marx's (1956) focus on economics, structural arguments, and ideas of dominance and dominant groups with the power to define social norms continues to shape definitions and conceptual frameworks. Similarly, Weber's concept of status groups whose members define consumption choices and monopolize social goods began a focus on the patterns of individuals rather than solely focusing on economic definitions of social class. That idea of individual patterns and choices, or agency, also molds definitions and conceptual frameworks.

Following Weber (1946), the term *socioeconomic status* denotes a wide range of stratified status characteristics and traits, even though empirical measures of it tend to be more restrictive (Theodorson and Theodorson, 1969). More often, however, the SES background of a student is operationalized by parental educational level, occupational status, and income, sometimes also combining items in the home, such as computers or books (Blau and Duncan, 1967; Sewell and Hauser, 1975; Blau, Duncan, and Tyree, 1994; Sewell, Haller, and Portes, 1994; Terenzini et al., 2001), thus incorporating Marxist (1956) ideas of economic position and Weberian (1946) consumption patterns. For students, SES historically was defined by the father's status on these variables, but in recent decades, the definition has also included the mother's educational level, occupational status, and income (Persell, Catsambis, and Cookson, 1992).

Many studies in higher education research have used measures of SES (Carnevale and Rose, 2004; Perna and Titus, 2004; Terenzini et al., 2001; Titus, 2006c; Walpole, 2003; Williams, Leppel, and Waldauer, 2005), typically consisting of a composite variable that combines parental education levels, parental income, and parental occupational status (Terenzini et al., 2001; Walpole, 2003). Although these three components are used together as SES, scholars have at times used individual components such as parental occupation (Slaney and Brown, 1983) or parental education (Goyette and Mullen, 2006) while still employing the term *SES* to define their students. Furthermore, each SES component is also used independently in higher education research. Several researchers have focused solely on parental or family income (Akerhielm et al., 1998; Paulsen and St. John, 2002; Perna, 2005; Teranishi et al., 2004), and others on parental education, which includes the study of first-generation students (Choy et al., 2000; Ishitani, 2006; Nunez and Cuccaro-Alamin, 1998; Pascarella et al., 2004; Rodriguez, 2003; Terenzini et al., 1996). Finally, scholars focusing on working-class students most often use parental occupation to define their participants, drawing solely on the third component of the SES variable (Casey, 2005; Goldstein, 1974; Littrell, 1999; Luzzo, 1992; O'Dair, 2003; Tett, 2004).

These four approaches (SES, parental income, parental education, and parental occupation) obviously address overlapping groups of students, and as will become evident, these groups face similar challenges in the educational system. Yet while first-generation students, who are defined by their parents' educational levels, clearly face trials similar to low-SES and low-income students, scholars typically do not explicitly describe these students as belonging to a larger group that includes low-SES and low-income students. Furthermore, within each of the four groups, individual studies and researchers operationalize these definitions differently. The following sections illustrate the diversity of definitions used in research on this population of students.

Defining Socioeconomic Status

In defining SES, both Terenzini and colleagues (2001) and Walpole (2003) employed a combination of parental education, parental income, and parental occupational status, while Goyette and Mullen (2006) operationalized parents' SES using parental education only, and Slaney and Brown (1983) defined SES using parental occupation solely. So although these scholars all used the term *SES*, they operationalized it quite differently. Moreover, Dennis, Phinney, and Chuateco (2005) defined their students by using SES and parental education by including a relative SES measure in their study of first-generation college students. Their SES measure was a composite based on parental education and occupational status. Low-SES parental education was indicated by less than a high school diploma and unskilled occupations, medium SES encompassed parents with a high school diploma but no college experience with skilled occupations, and students from high-SES families had at least one parent with some college experience, but no parents with a college diploma, which is how the authors defined first-generation status. The high-SES parents had what the authors referred to as white-collar or professional occupations, but they did not provide definitions or a scale used to determine how to categorize parental occupation. Furthermore, several national longitudinal data sets have been employed that contain SES measures, and these definitions also differ from one another.

Williams et al. (2005) used the Beginning Postsecondary Students (BPS) data set in which parents' occupation, items in the home, and family income were the items in the composite SES variable. BPS also included a separate measure of cultural resources, which inquired about daily newspaper subscriptions, encyclopedia ownership, and number of books in the home. Davies and Guppy (1997) used the National Longitudinal Survey of Youth (NLSY) data set. That data set also employed a composite variable for SES but included father's socio-economic index and parents' educational attainment. NLSY's separate measure of cultural resources includes magazine subscriptions, newspaper subscriptions, and library card possession as items. Titus (2006c) used BPS 96/01, and also used a composite for SES calculated from parental income and educational attainment. In a second study, Titus (2006b) used BPS 96/01 again and included a measure of parental wealth in addition to parental income and parental education (which were separate variables rather than combined into an SES composite score). High School and Beyond (HSandB) and the National Education Longitudinal Survey (NELS:88) both contained a composite SES score based on reported income, parental education, and parental occupation (Carnevale and Rose, 2004). Beattie (2002) used the HSandB data set, and the SES consisted of five items: family income, father's occupation, father's education, mother's education, and household possession index.

Moreover, some scholars disagree about whether using a composite measure of SES is appropriate. Terenzini and his colleagues (2001) recommended employing composite scores for SES rather than relying on a single measure. They provided a detailed analysis of the multiple variables used in how SES is constructed and why it is a more robust variable than using a single measure or a combination of other measures. Paulsen and St. John (2002), however, criticized the use of SES, claiming it fails to adequately account for the complex nature of how social status, income, and education level synthesize to explain educational outcomes.

Definitions of Parental Income

Instead of SES, Paulsen and St. John (2002) used four income categories to examine students' college choice and persistence within the financial nexus model. In addition, students from low-income families have received the focus of several other higher education researchers employing parental income as a stand-alone variable (Akerhielm et al., 1998; DesJardin, Ahlburg, and McCall, 2006; Perna, 2005; Teranishi et al., 2004). Low-income students in the Paulsen and St. John study reported family incomes of $11,000 or less, while lower-middle-income students had income higher than $11,000 but less than $30,000. Middle-income students' family income was at least $30,000 but less than $60,000, and high-income students had incomes equal to or above $60,000. Perna (2005) also employed income quartiles in her study of the economic benefits of higher education. Akerhielm and coauthors (1998) used NELS data (which has a composite SES variable) and categorized data into three groups—low, middle, and top income—with approximately the same percentage of students in each group. Teranishi and his colleagues (2004) employed Cooperative Institutional Research Program (CIRP) data and defined income on a four-point scale: low income as less than $25,000 per year, two middle categories (which were not used in the analysis) with ranges of $25,000 to $49,999 and $50,000 to $74,999, and high income as above $75,000 per year. DesJardin and colleagues' (2006) income scale was more complex than the others. It was a ten-point scale ranging from less than $18,000 to above $100,000, at the lower end consisting of intervals of $6,000, middle intervals of $8,000 and $10,000, and upper intervals of $20,000. Related to income, Titus (2006b) also included measures of family wealth in his analysis and found that this addition provided additional analytical insights.

Parental Education Definitions

In addition to parental income, parental education is often included in SES, although it is sometimes used as a single variable defining SES (Goyette and Mullen, 2006). In addition, parental education is a factor that defines first-generation students, but even within this group of studies, scholars have used differing definitions (Choy et al., 2000; Ishitani, 2006; Nunez and Cuccaro-Alamin, 1998; Pascarella et al., 2004; Pike and Kuh, 2005; Rodriguez, 2003; Terenzini et al., 1996). Many scholars have focused on this group, and most of the studies defined first-generation students as those whose parents did not have above a high school diploma (Choy et al., 2000; Ishitani, 2006; Nunez and Cuccaro-Alamin, 1998; Pascarella et al., 2004; Rodriguez, 2003; Terenzini et al., 1996). One study defined a first-generation student as one who did not have a parent or guardian with a bachelor's degree (Pike and Kuh, 2005). Filkins and Doyle (2002) did not specify their definition of a first-generation student.

Definitions of Parental Occupation

Parental occupation is a third component of a composite SES variable that also is used independently in some studies. Although occasionally used solely as a definition of SES (Slaney and Brown, 1983), studies that look at parental occupation are more often focused on working-class students. In recent higher education research, studies employing students' class locations have been undertaken mostly by European researchers, particularly those from the United Kingdom (Archer and Hutchings, 2000; Ball, Reay, and David, 2002; Cabrito, 2004; Connor, 2001; Egerton, 2001; Egerton and Halsey, 1993; Lynch and O'Riordan, 1998; Marks, Turner, and Osborne, 2003; Tett, 2004). Once again, researchers have operationalized this variable in different ways. The self-identified working-class students in Tett's qualitative study (2004), conducted at an elite Scottish university, were classified as working class by the registrar and were the first in their families to attend university. Goldstein (1974) defined working-class students as those who self-reported that their fathers had no education beyond high school and worked in manual labor positions. Upper-middle-class students' fathers had college degrees from prestigious institutions and worked in professional capacities. Luzzo (1992) defined social class using parents' occupational status on the Duncan Index; Slaney and Brown (1983) used the same scale but employed the term *socioeconomic status.* Three authors—Casey (2005), Littrell (1999), and O'Dair (2003)—did not explicitly define *working class,* and Casey used the terms *first generation* and *working class* interchangeably. Clearly these scholars operationalized students' class locations in multiple ways. There is not a single unified definition used in research, and some authors do not define their uses.

Definitional Disunity

What is clear from these definitions is that researchers have used parental education, occupation, and income, solely or in combination, to define particular groups of students for study. In higher education scholarship, research using these definitions frequently focuses on low-SES, low-income, first-generation, and working-class students and has often been carried out in reference to other studies using a similar focus. So research on low-SES students references other studies on low-SES students without incorporating the research on first-generation students. First-generation student research, in turn, does not reference research on working-class students. The net effect is that these research areas become de facto silos, each often isolated from the others, even though the students in each category often face similar challenges in their access to and completion of college.

In addition, the diversity of definitions, even within each area, makes within-group comparisons difficult. For example, a category Paulsen and St. John (2002) define as lower middle includes a range that Teranishi and colleagues (2004) split into low income and middle income. At the opposite end of the continuum, some of the students whom Paulsen and St. John consider as high income, Teranishi et al. instead consider to be middle income. Dennis and colleagues (2005) defined high-SES students as having parents with some college education but no degree, a definition that is clearly difficult to compare with other studies' results for high-SES students. It would be relatively easy for educators who are not trained in research methods to peruse these studies and come to the conclusion that there is no clear pattern in SES effects. This is not the case.

Individual researchers need to choose definitions that are suitable to their studies, and I think it would be futile, misleading, and counterproductive to have a single definition or single set of definitions for such a heterogeneous group of students. Nevertheless, I think it is important that researchers situate their studies in a larger context of similar studies to ease readers' synthesis and ease practitioners' applications. Recognizing and addressing the overlap in these areas of research furthers understandings of the similarities and differences among these students.

Umbrella Term

Although I do not think a single definition is appropriate, since the research on low-SES, low-income, first-generation, and working-class students clearly overlaps conceptually, if not operationally, I propose creating a broader category to include all the research on this population. Referencing other studies' definitions and findings, as well as viewing students' experiences holistically, may provide new insights that will assist policymakers and practitioners. I propose the term *economically and educationally challenged* (EEC) to describe these students. Although not all economically challenged students are educationally challenged and not all those who come from families with lower levels of formal education are economically challenged, this collective group of EEC students faces similar obstacles in gaining access to college, reports similar kinds of experiences and levels of involvement while enrolled, and has similar outcomes after college. I want to be clear that these students confront challenges and have different, and often lower, success rates than students who do not face similar challenges, not because they lack ability, motivation, or are somehow deficient. Rather, these students must cope with a structure and a system that defines merit in ways that do not privilege them (Bowen et al., 2005; Karabel, 2005; McNamee and Miller, 2004).

I believe that by thinking of, reading about, and referencing this broader EEC category, we may learn from one another; push forward our collective thinking, practices, and policy recommendations; and begin to make progress in our quest for better access, persistence, and outcomes for these students. Thus I will incorporate the term *EEC* in the remainder of this volume when referencing the broadly defined students the term incorporates. We must find ways to understand and reduce the 30 percent gap in college attendance (Bedsworth et al., 2006), and combining the studies in this area under such an umbrella term may provide connections that help foster such a reduction in addition to increasing the percentage of low-SES students who actually attain a degree, which currently stands at a paltry one student in seven.

Another advantage to such a term is solidarity and possible political mobilization. Karen (1991) and more recently Karabel (2005) both believe that part of the reason this student population has not attracted more attention, resources, and solutions is a lack of political mobilization. In contrast to other groups that have been able to make some gains by collectively drawing attention to the inequities they experience, low-SES, low-income, first-generation, and working-class students have not done so. A lack of a collective identity has been a stumbling block in their mobilization. Although a collective umbrella term would not necessarily assist students in gaining a collective identity, it could help scholars and practitioners seek resources for research and programming.

Finally, such an umbrella term could also lead to new theoretical insights. Similar to the multiple definitions are the several conceptual approaches and models that scholars use. These approaches and models are linked to many of the definitions and are based on several different academic disciplines. While this is appropriate in a multidisciplinary field such as higher education, it too can contribute to the fragmentation of research findings on these students. In ways similar to the definitional silos, researchers often reference prior work done in the area using the same conceptual framework or disciplinary approach. An umbrella term defining these students could highlight the research on these students from every theoretical or disciplinary approach, which may provide new conceptual insights in addition to increased access and attainment. We now turn to some of the more frequently used frameworks and models.

Conceptual Approaches

IN ADDITION TO THE MULTIPLE DEFINITIONS RESEARCHERS have used, a number of theoretical or conceptual approaches, frameworks, and models have guided recent research on social class in higher education. This chapter provides an overview of these conceptual frameworks: the status attainment model (Blau and Duncan, 1967; Carter, 1999; Sewell and Hauser, 1975), human capital theory (Beattie, 2002; Becker, 1993; Long, 2007; Perna, 2005), the financial nexus model (Paulsen and St. John, 1997, 2002), Bourdieu's framework (Bourdieu, 1977; Horvat, 2001; McDonough, 1997; McDonough, Ventresca, and Outcault, 2000; Walpole, 2003), and critical race theory (Ladson-Billings, 2005; Ladson-Billings and Tate, 1995; Tate, 1997; Solorzano and Bernal, 2001; Solorzano and Villalpando, 1998; Yosso, 2005). These frameworks appropriately draw on several disciplinary traditions, including sociology, psychology, and economics, because higher education research is multidisciplinary. Furthermore, the definitions and the conceptual approaches and models are clearly linked. This linkage is to be expected because the ways in which scholars think about and define problems and questions also shape their approaches and models. Two concepts, structure and agency, clearly echo throughout the definitions and the conceptual approaches and models. I believe one of the most challenging scholarly tasks facing researchers, policymakers, and practitioners is to account for the ways in which agency and structure contribute to students' decisions and eventual attainment.

The frameworks focus on how structural forces in society, such as economic forces, families, schools, and communities, shape social class attainment; how individual choices, also referred to as agency, affect a person's socioeconomic status; or how the two are combined in order to understand outcomes. The focus on structural forces and agency incorporates earlier understandings of the complexities of social class and social standing in the U.S. context, echoing both Marx's (1956) and Weber's (1946) seminal definitions. Understanding the focus of each framework and the potential contributions will help provide a more holistic understanding of the ways in which social class affects college admissions, experiences, and outcomes.

Status Attainment Models

Sociologists have long studied how social class differences shape educational and occupational outcomes, as well as social mobility. College students from low-SES backgrounds are seen as upwardly socially mobile, which means they are changing their class status from the status into which they were born (Theodorson and Theodorson, 1969). As part of an international effort to examine intergenerational social mobility (Blau, 1992), Blau and Duncan (1967) investigated mobility in the United States. Their work in 1967 illustrated that status attainment is a life-long process, predicated in large part by educational attainment (Blau et al., 1994; Corcoran, 1995; Pascarella and Terenzini, 1991, 2005). Their model predicted the adult occupational status of their respondents based on four variables: father's occupational status, father's education, respondent's educational level, and status of the respondent's first job (Blau and Duncan, 1967; Blau et al., 1994). These variables focused on explaining structural factors in occupational status and did not include variables accounting for individual choice or agency (Carter, 1999). They found evidence for substantial intergenerational mobility, mobility positively affected by educational attainment. They also found that the SES of origin, although an important influence, did not uniformly predict the SES of adulthood.

Despite the model's wide acceptance, Sewell and Hauser (1975) viewed the Blau and Duncan (1967) model as incomplete, choosing to incorporate ability, aspirations, and the influence of significant others into subsequent status attainment models (Sewell and Hauser, 1975; Sewell et al., 1994). While they identified educational attainment as a significant factor in eventual status attainment, they noted that the influence of significant others and individuals' aspirations mediated educational attainment. Sewell and Hauser further posited that educational aspirations worked as nonlinear independent forces on educational attainment as well as having a mediating influence. They believed that when this nonlinear effect occurred, the effects of parental backgrounds, significant others, and ability on aspiration formation could accelerate over time, facilitating early adulthood educational attainment.

Despite the seminal nature of these studies, Corcoran (1995) criticized them for using cross-sectional rather than longitudinal data; for focusing on White, employed men; and for viewing family structure in ways that did not account for variation, especially because they did not look at female-headed households. In addition, the studies have been criticized for not accounting for the role of individual agency in attainment (Carter, 1999). Conley (2001) noted that the model did not include a measure of family wealth, but he found that wealth had a significant independent effect on college enrollment and completion.

Jencks and colleagues (1972, 1994) supported the findings of intergenerational mobility, yet they criticized these early models for viewing mobility and prosperity in absolute terms; Jencks and his colleagues pointed out that Americans viewed their prosperity and the prosperity of others in historically based relative terms. These researchers believed that during times of economic growth, Americans held differing definitions of the income, occupational status, and educational attainment required for inclusion in specific social strata (Jencks et al., 1972, 1994); this meant that the power of income or educational attainment gains made by people at the lower ends of the socioeconomic strata could be reduced if similar or greater gains were made by those in the upper strata. Therefore, in investigating social mobility, Jencks and his colleagues suggested concentrating on the relative socioeconomic gains of those from low-SES backgrounds compared to high-SES backgrounds rather than focusing on absolute gains.

More recently, Carter (1999) used status attainment models as her theoretical foundation for examining degree expectations of White and African American students, focusing on SES and academic ability as variables that affected the encouragement and support a student receives, which then shaped aspirations and expectations. Her findings generally supported the Sewell and Hauser (1975) models, with SES and contact with faculty and peers significantly predicting students' degree expectations.

These early status attainment models illustrated that family socioeconomic status can play an important role in social mobility (Blau and Duncan, 1967; Blau et al., 1994; Sewell and Hauser, 1975; Sewell et al., 1994) and provided a base for other theorists to build on. Using these models, researchers have found that intergenerational mobility was possible and that educational attainment, the influence of others, and aspirations played key roles. The researchers were criticized because they failed to include important additional factors, such as race, gender, and family structure, as well as individual agency, which may influence the transmission of intergenerational class status. Later theorists sought to address these concerns.

Human Capital Theory

Human capital theory has used an economic lens in studies of education and class stratification. This theory assumes that students considering postsecondary education make their choices based on rational economic factors (Beattie, 2002; Becker, 1993; Long, 2007; Perna, 2005). These theorists believed students weigh the costs of postsecondary education, including tuition, fees, books, room and board, commuting costs, lost wages, and psychic costs, against the perceived economic and psychic benefits that will come with a degree. Thus, this theoretical lens has focused almost exclusively on individual choice, or agency. The scholars using the framework have subscribed to the concept that educational attainment directly affected subsequent productivity and income.

Beattie's study (2002) using this framework looked at how the economic returns of college varied for different groups and how students' decisions were affected by the economic differentials. She found that low-SES men's enrollment in higher education was most closely aligned with the framework. Perna (2000a, 2000b, 2004) and Perna and Titus (2004) employed a modified human capital theory that incorporated cultural and social capital with economic capital to understand stratification in higher education. Long (2007) recently reviewed the economic literature focused on higher education, including access, persistence, and outcomes. Many of the studies she reviewed employed human capital theory and found general support for human capital theoretical tenets. Heller and Rasmussen's (2002) study on state merit scholarships in Florida and Michigan also used human capital theory as one of their theoretical frameworks.

Financial Nexus Model

The financial nexus model has linked economic models and student behavior to gain insight into how students' financial perceptions and realities shaped their college choice decisions and persistence (St. John, Cabrera, Nora, and Asker, 2000). Research on persistence has historically had an economic strand, linking persistence to financial factors (Astin, 1975; Cabrera, Nora, and Castaneda, 1992; St. John and Starkey, 1995), and a strand focused on how the fit between the student and the institution affects persistence (Tinto, 1987, 1993). Linking these strands, the financial nexus model evolved empirically from efforts to connect research on the economic influences of persistence to research on how student-institution fit influenced student persistence, adding college choice decisions to the two strands (St. John et al., 2000). Thus, the model has incorporated both structural factors and individual agency in explicating the relationships of financial considerations, college choice, and persistence (Hwang, 2003; Paulsen and St. John, 1997, 2002; St. John, Paulsen, and Carter, 2005).

The model considered the financial variables that formed a context for students' decisions, affecting both the initial college enrollment decision and the subsequent persistence or attrition decision, and has been used to compare groups of students (St. John et al., 2005). The model also explicitly explored the decisions of students who were considered nontraditional, including African American and low-SES students (Paulsen and St. John, 1997, 2002; St. John et al., 2005). In addition, Paulsen and St. John's 2002 model overtly linked the financial nexus model to Bourdieu's (1977, 1990, 1994) framework.

Bourdieu's Framework

Bourdieu (1977, 1990, 1994) employed the concepts of cultural capital, social capital, and habitus to explain the ways in which individual agency, or choice, combined with socially structured opportunities, such as college admission, to reproduce the existing social structure. Working in France during the middle of the twentieth century, a time when social science clearly dichotomized structural factors and individual agency in explaining social class and social structure, Bourdieu sought to reconcile the two and illuminate the inextricable linkages between them in understanding social class, connecting theory to empirical data (Horvat, 2001). Moreover, Bourdieu denounced the agency-structure dichotomy as false, combining structural factors and individual agency to explain the reproduction of existing social stratification (Horvat, 2001, 2003). This sociological framework has been significant in higher education research and to this volume because it explicitly focuses on explaining social class reproduction as mediated by educational institutions.

Bourdieu's framework (1977, 1990, 1994) defines several types of capital. In addition to economic capital, each social class possesses social and cultural capital, which parents pass on to their children as attitudes, preferences, and behaviors that are invested for social profits (Lamont and Lareau, 1988). Knowledge of the college admissions process and behaviors that increase a student's chances of being admitted to a particular institution are examples of cultural capital (McDonough, 1997). Accumulating cultural capital in a Bourdieuian framework is most useful for its conversion potential. Educational decisions and choices are made in an attempt to accumulate this capital, which may be converted at a future date in pursuit of further educational and occupational gains (Lareau, 1993; MacLeod, 1987; McDonough, Antonio, and Trent, 1997; Walpole, 2003).

While each social class possesses a distinct cultural capital, the most valuable is the cultural capital of the dominant classes, which is not taught explicitly in schools (Bourdieu, 1990). Although this capital is not taught in schools, educators differentially value this dominant cultural capital, rewarding students from high-SES backgrounds who possess it, leaving low-SES students at risk for lower success rates in school. This differential valuing of high-status cultural capital by educational professionals results in further dominant cultural capital accumulation in the form of educational credentials during the process of schooling (Bourdieu, 1994). This dominant capital accumulation is displayed disproportionately by high-SES students in the form of high grades and test scores, admission to prestigious universities and graduate schools, and degrees obtained. In a Bourdieuian framework, then, cultural capital is a structuring mechanism for educational outcomes. Yet this framework does not exclusively privilege structuring mechanisms such as cultural capital, instead focusing on how the nexus between structure and individual agency shapes educational outcomes.

Bourdieu's framework views individuals as status strivers who strategically improvise to attain desired social and economic goods (McDonough, Ventresca, and Outcault, 2000), and that improvisation is regulated by the habitus (Bourdieu, 1977). Habitus acts as a web of perceptions regarding opportunities and the possible and appropriate responses in any situation; people from the same social class often have common perceptions and responses, which comprise individual agency (Berger, Milem, and Paulsen, 1998; Bourdieu, 1977; Horvat, 2001; McDonough, 1997). This agency, or habitus, works at the subconscious level in tandem with structural realities to shape educational outcomes.

Habitus has two facets. The durable nature of the low-SES student's habitus would lead that student to have lower aspirations as well as predispose the student to use educational strategies that may not be as successful in attaining the desired social profits (McDonough, 1997; Walpole, 2003). The durable nature of the habitus could also lead students to resist adopting new habitus elements. In fact, previous studies of resistance using a Bourdieuian framework have found resistance to be self-defeating, resulting in the maintenance of a lower social position (MacLeod, 1987; Willis, 1977). However, the transposable nature of habitus means that a low-SES student can adopt new values, or habitus elements, as a result of novel experiences, historical changes in the material environment, or exposure to another individual's habitus, which are possible in the college environment (Harker, 1984; Horvat, 2001; Lamont and Lareau, 1988). These new elements may contribute to upward mobility. These decisions to resist or adopt new elements are not conscious; rather, they are based on nonconscious perceptions of what feels natural, normal, or right in a particular situation; those perceptions in turn are rooted in social class and social status. Resolving the tension between the durable and transposable natures of the habitus may be addressed through improvisation, but the resolution of that tension and the role of improvisation are underdeveloped in the framework (McDonough et al., 2000).

Several studies in higher education have adopted a Bourdieuian framework (McDonough, 1997; Walpole, 2003, in press; Walpole, McDonough, Bauer, Gibson, Kanyi, and Toliver, 2005) or a modified Bourdieuian framework (Paulsen and St. John, 2002; Perna, 2000a, 2000b; Perna and Titus, 2004). The terms *cultural capital* and *social capital* are in fact widely used (Hamrick and Stage, 2004; Lareau and Weininger, 2003; Pascarella et al., 2004) and are almost ubiquitous. Yet these terms are often used in isolation from the totality of Bourdieu's framework. In addition, Bourdieu's concept of social capital as an individual possession valuable for its conversion potential (Horvat, 2001) is often confused and conflated with Coleman's concept (1988) of the social capital found in networks and communities.

Despite the widespread use of Bourdieu's concepts (1977, 1990, 1994), or at least his terms, his work has been criticized as deterministic and for privileging the cultural capital possessed by elite social groups over that possessed by nonelite groups (Yosso, 2005). However, according to Bourdieu (1990), the value of capital is arbitrary and is set by those in dominant social and educational positions who differentially value particular types of cultural capital, especially those of elite groups, which then form the basis of exclusivity, clearly reflecting the influences of Marx (1956) and Weber (1946). In fact, Bourdieu (1990) believes it is only because the dominant elite have the power to define what is valued and what is not, and because educational systems reflect those values, that students from particular backgrounds experience more or less success in educational institutions. Bourdieu aims to describe social structure as it exists and to describe its reproduction in conjunction with schools (Horvat, 2001, 2003).

Critical Race Theory

In criticizing Bourdieu's work, Yosso (2005) highlights the strengths of another theoretical framework, critical race theory (CRT), which was imported to education from a legal framework rooted in the civil rights movement (Ladson-Billings, 2005; Ladson-Billings and Tate, 1995; Tate, 1997). This theory provides new insights into the educational experiences of students who are underrepresented in higher education and has important implications for understanding the experiences of EEC students.

Ladson-Billings and Tate (1995) believe that the issue of race is undertheorized in educational research and that inequitable educational experiences and outcomes are "a logical and predictable result of a racialized society" (p. 47). They predicate their theoretical framework on three arguments. First, race is a defining feature of inequality; second, rights in the United States are strongly rooted in rights based on property; and third, the combination of race and property rights provides a theoretical lens through which to understand inequality. In this framework, curriculum and Whiteness are examples of property that are used to create educational inequality (Ladson-Billings and Tate, 1995). For example, a CRT analysis of affirmative action views legal challenges to affirmative action as a method of protecting the property of Whiteness and White privilege (Dixson and Rousseau, 2005). Although this framework focuses on racial inequality, Tate (2005) recently called for scholars to incorporate socioeconomic differences into CRT to understand how resource differences combine with structural racism to perpetuate educational inequalities.

Although relatively new, this framework is also providing important theoretical insights into understanding the educational experiences of underrepresented students, particularly in colleges and universities. Critical race theory is significant because it recognizes resistance to the hegemony of middle- and upper-middle-class White culture as a potential positive force in the educational attainment of a dominated group, and not necessarily as always a negative, self-defeating force (Solorzano and Bernal, 2001; Solorzano and Villalpando, 1998; Teranishi, 2002). By embracing their marginal status, students can use their position as a source of knowledge, empowerment, liberation, or transformation (Solorzano and Bernal, 2001; Solorzano and Villalpando, 1998). Furthermore, the Latino students in these studies at times acquired dominant cultural capital and conformed to the norms of the cultural hegemony, while resisting it at other times. In particular, theorists have conceptualized this resistance as a type of cultural capital, including resources from family stories, proverbs, and oral histories that nondominant group students may use to affirm their group identity and empower themselves (Solorzano and Villalpando, 1998; Yosso, 2005). This resistant cultural capital may provide culturally congruent methods for achieving success in college (McDonough, Nunez, Ceja, and Solarzano, 2003). Thus, resistance in the CRT framework works to reconcile social mobility through educational attainment with cultural preservation. Moreover, self-definition, voice, and storytelling are explicit tenets of CRT, allowing dominated groups to illuminate structural inequities and soothe wounds caused by them (Ladson-Billings and Tate, 1995).

Although not as explicitly as in Bourdieu's framework, CRT incorporates both structural factors and individual choice. The framework is predicated on a belief in structural racism and seeks to make the racist structure of society visible (Ladson-Billings and Tate, 1995; Tate, 1997). However, the work on students' experiences within this racialized structure, and their decisions to conform to and resist such a structure, incorporates individual agency (Solorzano and Bernal, 2001; Solorzano and Villalpando, 1998).

Conclusion

Although distinct, each of these conceptual approaches provides linkages to understanding low-SES, low-income, working-class, and first-generation (EEC) students. Moreover, frameworks have become increasingly complex in an effort to understand and account for the multiple and overlapping factors that affect students' opportunities and decisions. That increasing complexity attempts to account for both structure and agency (Bourdieu, 1977, 1990, 1994; Ladson-Billings, 2005; Ladson-Billings and Tate, 1995; Paulsen and St. John, 1997, 2002; St. John et al., 2000, St. John et al., 2005; Solorzano and Bernal, 2001; Solorzano and Villalpando, 1998; Tate, 1997). Students' experiences and decisions reflect a complex array of factors. About some, they make conscious or unconscious decisions, such as majors or level of involvement; over some, such as discrimination and financial factors, they have little control. It is important to have theoretical frameworks that can account for the totality of students' experiences, decisions, and outcomes.

Clearly the frameworks reviewed here are not yet able to meet that accountability standard. However, researchers employing the financial nexus model, the Bourdieuian framework, and CRT are all working to incorporate both structure and agency and address the complex realities of students' lived experiences. The financial nexus model has evolved empirically to join research strands focused on persistence in an effort to more fully understand the subject. Paulsen and St. John (2002) have since linked the financial nexus model to Bourdieu's framework. Perna, (2000a, 2000b; 2006) and Perna and Titus (2004) have incorporated Bourdieuian concepts into human capital theory. Perna (2006) proposed a conceptual framework that incorporates not only sociological and economic aspects, but also multiple contexts, including the school, higher education, and policy contexts. Moreover, recent efforts have begun linking Bourdieu's framework and CRT (Nunez et al., 2004; Walpole, 2004). Such efforts to empirically evolve and link theories and frameworks will continue to advance our understanding regarding EEC students. As such attempts continue, the challenge for theorists and researchers will be to balance the complexities students experience with the need for analytical and explanatory power.

It is important to note that some of these frameworks and models align more easily with particular methodological approaches and data collection strategies. In recent higher education research, status attainment theory (Carter, 1999), human capital theory (Beattie, 2002; Perna, 2000a, 2000b; Perna and Titus, 2004), the financial nexus model (Paulsen and St. John, 2002; St. John et al., 2005), and Bourdieu's work (Walpole, 2003) have been explored with quantitative methods. Bourdieu's theory has also been employed in qualitative work (McDonough, 1997; Walpole et al., 2005), as has CRT (Solorzano and Bernal, 2001; Solorzano and Villalpando, 1998; Teranishi, 2002). Nunez and her coauthors (2004) explored the use of both a Bourdieuian framework and CRT in a quantitative study of the role of ethnicity in Latino students' college choice. Researchers should also continue to look for new methodological approaches that may provide information to assist in understanding and improving EEC students' access, persistence, and outcomes.

EEC students' experiences and outcomes are a multifaceted, interrelated, and synergistic combination of structural factors and individual decisions. Developing a framework that can simultaneously account for the complexity of incorporating structure as well as agency and can be operationalized in study designs is a significant challenge that, when met, will help ensure equity in educational institutions. In higher education, that equity begins with preparation for college and college admission, and we turn our attention to those topics next.

College Access and Admission

ECONOMICALLY AND EDUCATIONALLY CHALLENGED students' trials begin long before they enroll in college, and we now examine college access and admission for this group of students, a topic that has been explored in more depth than either college experiences or outcomes. These studies are grouped by the ways in which they define students' parental SES, income, education, or occupation. I also highlight the particular theoretical or disciplinary approaches when possible. Several of the reviewed studies were research reports, and so did not employ a conceptual framework or offer explanations for findings, simply reporting them instead. Moreover, in some of the scholarly studies, the authors did not employ theory to explain their results, and so it was not always possible to highlight such an approach.

The documentation of social class differences in students' college choice processes, college attendance rates, and the types of colleges they attend, is replete with evidence showing that EEC students are less likely to attend college and more likely to attend a less selective institution when they do enroll in college than are more advantaged students (Astin and Oseguera, 2004; Bedsworth et al., 2006; Bowen et al., 2005; Cabrera et al., 2005; Hearn, 1984, 1990, 1991; Karabel, 2005; Karabel and Astin, 1975; Karen, 1991; McDonough, 1997; Tinto, 2006; Titus, 2006a, 2006c). The fact that EEC students disproportionately attend less selective colleges has long-term consequences, as these institutions have lower graduation rates and graduate school attendance rates than more selective colleges (Anderson and Hearn, 1992; Astin, 1993, 1999; Astin and Oseguera, 2004; Borrego, 2001; Bowen et al., 2005; Carnevale and Rose, 2004; Hearn, 1984,

1990, 1991; Karabel, 2005; McDonough, 1997; Terenzini et al., 2001; Tinto, 2006; Titus, 2006b, 2006c). There are multiple reasons for these differences that occur prior to students' applying for and enrolling in college, including familial considerations, organizational obstacles, and individual agency.

Prior Educational Experiences

Parental expectations and definitions of success vary with social status and mediate student aspirations. In research focused specifically on SES, several researchers found that low-SES parents are more likely to view a high school diploma as the norm for their children than are high-SES parents, to whom a bachelor's or advanced degree is considered the norm (Halle, 1984; Lareau, 1987, 1993; MacLeod, 1987; McDonough, 1997; Rubin, 1976; Sennett and Cobb, 1973; Willis, 1977). To these low-SES parents, college attendance is often at a local community college or technical school (Rubin, 1976). In contrast, high-SES parents define success for their children as four years of college attendance and, more recently, attendance at a "good" college (Bowen et al., 2005; Karabel, 2005; Lareau, 1987, 1993; McDonough, 1997; Rubin, 1976).

Low-SES students disproportionately attend high schools that do not focus on preparing students for college and have fewer counseling resources (McDonough, 1997). In addition, low-SES and low-income students are more likely than high-SES and high-income students to lack access to rigorous course work and to be tracked away from honors and advanced placement courses (Adelman, 2006; Akerhielm et al., 1998; Cabrera and La Nasa, 2000a; Martin, Karabel, and Jaquez, 2005; Oakes, 1985; Perna, 2000a; Terenzini et al., 2001). Several studies have demonstrated that schools direct low-SES students toward vocational programs and away from college preparatory courses in high schools, resulting in lower attainment (Cicourel and Kitsuse, 1963; Gaskell, 1985; MacLeod, 1987; Willis, 1977). Moreover, low-SES, working-class, and first-generation students have fewer resources and less knowledge about the admissions process or the differences among college types (Cabrera and La Nasa, 2000b; Choy et al., 2000; Freeman, 1997, 1999; Horvat, 1996a, 1996b, 1997, 2003; Lynch and O'Riordan, 1998; Martin et al., 2005; McDonough, 1997; Terenzini et al., 2001; Walpole et al., 2005).

In contrast, due to high-quality academic preparation and by using several strategies, students without economic and educational challenges gain access to universities, and particularly to elite institutions, at higher rates than their EEC peers (Astin, 1993; Bowen et al., 2005; Cookson and Persell, 1985; Domhoff, 1983; Hearn, 1990, 1991; Karabel, 2005; Kingston and Smart, 1990; Martin et al., 2005; McDonough, 1994, 1997; Persell and Cookson, 1990; Persell et al., 1992; Zweigenhaft and Domhoff, 1991). These strategies include hedging their admission bets by applying to large numbers of colleges, using test preparation services to improve their entrance exam scores, and employing private consultants to assist with admissions packaging (McDonough, 1994). All of these strategies consume considerable investments of time and money, neither of which EEC students possess in abundance.

Research specifically focused on low-SES students found that these students are less likely than their peers to view college as a realistic option and are more likely to see employment options as more comfortable (Akerhielm et al., 1998; Freeman, 1997, 1999; MacLeod, 1987; Tett, 2004; Willis, 1977). In an interview in 2004, Levine stated that for poor children, "education is a ritual without consequence. It is disconnected from advancement in the real world in which they live" (Where are the poor students? 2004, p. 20). Archer and Hutchings (2000) interviewed young working-class people who were not in college and found that they believed the risks and uncertainties of attending college outweighed the promised economic benefits. The risks included failing academically as well as risks to their working-class identities. Connor (2001) surveyed and interviewed students from a wide variety of social class backgrounds about their decisions to attend university and found that young people who did not enroll cited wanting to work and earn money and fear of student loans as reasons not to enroll. Marks et al. (2003) found that their English and Scottish subjects viewed higher education as an intimidating reserve for the wealthy.

Socioeconomic Status

Whatever the reasons, research has consistently found that low-SES students are less likely to aspire to, apply to, be prepared for, or enroll in postsecondary education than higher-SES students (Akerhielm et al., 1998; Carnevale and

Rose, 2004; Hossler and Maple, 1993; McDonough, 1997; Swail, Cabrera, and Lee, 2004; Terenzini et al., 2001; Tinto, 2006). Terenzini et al.'s study (2001) incorporated data from several national longitudinal data sets and found that low-SES students are disadvantaged at every step of the college choice process. In addition, they are more likely to delay college entry after high school, which lowers their likelihood of completing college, according to findings employing NELS 1988–2000 data (Goldrick-Rab and Han, 2006; Rowan, 2006).

Using a Bourdieuian framework, McDonough (1997) found that students' subjective assessments combined with the high school organizational habitus and class-based norms and expectations to form a web of opportunities that shaped the educational decisions of her participants. Controlling for academic ability, McDonough qualitatively investigated the college choice process of young women at four high schools: an elite private boarding school, a high-SES public school, a private Catholic high school serving low-SES students, and a low-SES public school. Although all students wanted to attend college and were academically able to do so, their choices depended on class-based notions of what constituted an appropriate choice as defined by parents, peers, and the organizational structure of the high school guidance process.

Cabrera and La Nasa (2000b, 2001), also using NELS:88 data, found that the low-SES students who completed three tasks were the most likely to enroll in a four-year college or university: achieving minimal academic qualifications, completing high school, and applying to college. However, less than a third of low-SES students, compared to 80 percent of high-SES students, completed the minimum academic requirements for college by the end of their senior year. Furthermore, just under three-quarters of low-SES students graduated from high school, as opposed to 98 percent of high-SES students. Finally, while over half of high-SES students enrolled in four-year institutions, less than 15 percent of low-SES students enrolled at those types of universities. Parental involvement in conjunction with school curricular policies that support students' obtaining college qualifications were critical in helping low-SES students complete a college preparatory curriculum in high school and enroll in college (Cabrera and La Nasa, 2000a, 2000c, 2001). Other scholars have found that parental involvement is a critical component of low-SES students' college enrollment (Hamrick and Stage, 2004; Perna, 2000b; Terenzini et al., 2001). Levine and Nidiffer (1996) found that mentors were critical in the lives of poor students who attended college. These mentors showed students the possibilities that education provided and guided them in the process.

Perna and Titus (2004) employed NELS 92/94 data, descriptive statistics, and hierarchical linear modeling (HLM) to demonstrate that low-SES students were less likely to enroll in college immediately following high school than high-SES students, even after controlling for academic achievement, state-level education policy, and financial aid factors. Using human capital theory modified by Bourdieuian concepts, they found that half (49 percent) of low-SES students did not make the transition to college after high school, a finding similar to that of Terenzini and colleagues (2001), while only 6.7 percent of high-SES students did not make the transition. Moreover, low-SES students were most likely to enroll in public two-year colleges when they did attend college. In analyzing the effects of state-level policies, Perna and Titus recommended keeping public sector tuition low and providing state-level aid based on need.

Low-SES students by definition have fewer financial resources available to them, and several studies found that they have more financial concerns than do their high-SES peers (Beattie, 2002; Terenzini et al., 2001). Terenzini and colleagues noted that low-SES students reported that financial aid was an important part of their choice more often than did their higher-SES peers at two-year and public four-year colleges, though not at private four-year institutions. They also reported that low-SES students' enrollments were very sensitive to tuition increases and found that financial aid was one of the most important reasons low-SES students cited when asked why they chose to attend a particular institution. Using the High School and Beyond database, Beattie (2002) concluded that male low-SES students and White, Asian, and Latino students were the most likely to enroll when costs were low and economic returns to educational attainment high, confirming the human capital theory they employed. African Americans students' enrollments were not affected by the economic returns to education. Women's results were mixed overall, but African American women and Latinas were more likely to enroll than were White women.

Parental Income

Several reports and studies have examined low-income students' access to college. Akerhielm and colleagues (1998) used parental income levels to explore postsecondary enrollment and found that low-income students were less likely to enter college than were high-income students, even when they had high test scores, were enrolled in rigorous academic programs, had taken advanced course work, and had taken algebra I in eighth grade. This research report employed NELS:88 and National Postsecondary Study Aid Survey (NPSAS) data and found that taking algebra I in eighth grade and advanced course work in high school did have a positive differential effect on low-income students, yet low-income students were less likely to take either algebra I in eighth grade or advanced course work in high school. Even when controlling for test scores, low-income students were less likely to attend college than high-income students. In addition, the study found that low-income students had lower educational aspirations in eighth grade and were more likely to report that they were not enrolling in college for financial reasons than did high-income students. Finally, they found that students from low-income families who had high test scores were the most likely to enter the armed forces after high school.

Bedsworth and his coauthors (2006) also focused on low-income students in their research report and used longitudinal NELS:88/2000 data. They similarly found that academic preparation is key to increasing the prospects of low-income youth attending college, but also found that students' expectations about the necessity of college preparation for their desired career was critical, increasing a student's chances of earning a degree by six times. They found that low-income students need more information about academic requirements and financial aid possibilities. Interestingly, although parental involvement was important, having a peer group that was planning on attending college was more important than parental encouragement.

Using data from students who sent ACT scores to one institution over a three-year period, a sample of almost 100,000 students, DesJardins et al. (2006) employed a series of probability estimates and concluded that low-income students were less likely to enroll across all racial and ethnic groups and that the expectation of aid, as well as the actual award received, affected their enrollment behaviors. Using the NPSAS data from 1987, Paulsen and

St. John (2002) identified financial factors as critical for low-income students' college choice and affected the types and locations of the institutions they attended. In their study, which incorporated the financial nexus model, low-income students also had lower aspirations than higher-income students.

Parental Education

According to Hossler, Schmit, and Vesper (1999), parental education levels, rather than income, shaped college aspirations and the students' abilities to realize their aspirations: students with more highly educated parents were more likely to aspire to and enroll in college than were students with less-well-educated parents. Hossler and Maple (1993) found that students with lower levels of parental education were less likely to plan to attend college. Similarly, Manski and Wise (1983) noted that higher parental education levels increased a student's odds of applying to a four-year college or university. These scholars also found an effect for parental income, although the effect was less pronounced than parental education. According to Hwang (2003), financial variables affected the college choices of some first-time, full-time college students, and specifically that students with more highly educated mothers were more likely to attend private institutions than were students whose mothers were less well educated.

First-generation students have parents who did not attend or complete college, and several scholars have examined these students. Gibbons and Shoffner (2004), in a case study design, illustrated how school officials could assist first-generation students in identifying and overcoming obstacles to applying to and enrolling in college. McCarron and Inkelas (2006) studied first-generation students' aspirations and found that socioeconomic status, students' perceptions of the importance of good grades, and parental involvement were significant predictors of students' aspirations. Seventy-eight percent of their sample of first-generation students fell into the lowest two SES quartiles. Gandara's qualitative study (1995) similarly found that parental involvement was a key for first-generation students' successful transition to college.

Using NELS data, Choy, Horn, Nunez, and Chen (2000) found that first-generation students were less likely to enroll in a four-year college than students whose parents had attended college. Examining the steps that students needed to take to understand why this population was less likely to enroll, they concluded that fewer than half of first-generation students aspired to a bachelor's degree in tenth grade and only a third acquired the minimum academic qualifications. In particular, first-generation students were less likely to have taken an advanced math curriculum, which is associated with enrolling in college. Nunez and Curraco-Alamin (1998) and Rouse (1994) found that first-generation students were more likely to attend two-year colleges and attend part time than were their non-first-generation peers.

Parental Occupation

Educators in the United States are not alone in their concern about the ways in which social class affects college enrollment. This issue has been explored for decades in other countries, particularly in the United Kingdom. Abbott (1965) wrote about the lack of working-class students in three universities in Britain. She has more recently been joined by a number of colleagues looking at inequities based on social class and how social class shapes access, experiences, and outcomes of higher education in Britain and Ireland (Archer and Hutchings, 2000; Ball, Reay, and David, 2002; Connor, 2001; Egerton, 2001; Egerton and Halsey, 1993; Lynch and O'Riordan, 1998; Marks et al., 2003; Shattock, 1981; Tett, 2004). Cabrito (2004) also documented the disproportionate lack of college enrollment for students from lower-class families in Portugal. Social class was defined in this and most other studies in the U.K. and Ireland by the father's occupational status.

Egerton and Halsey (1993) looked at enrollments in Britain by social class over a twenty-year period using a national database and saw that although access had increased, the gap between students from higher and lower social class backgrounds had not dissipated. Connor (2001) conducted a mixed-methods study including mailed surveys ($N = 1,667$), focus groups and individual interviews with first-year undergraduates at fourteen institutions, and telephone interviews with 176 similarly aged youth who did not attend college. For students from lower social class backgrounds in the United Kingdom, financial concerns were pressing issues in their decisions; her subjects were particularly concerned about financing their education. In Archer and Hutchings's study (2000), working-class youth in their focus groups believed college was risky and did not trust that they would benefit economically. They also worried about how college would change them as a person and whether they would continue to fit in with family and friends if they attended college. Ball et al. (2002) investigated ethnic minority students' college choice processes in Britain and found that parents' education played a significant role, with the students who did come from low-income, working-class families without a college education explicitly choosing to attend despite the obstacles. The conscious choice they found among the working class students was contrasted by students from families in which the parents had attended college, who assumed they would attend university; their choice was not a conscious one. Lynch and O'Riordan (1998) interviewed 122 people, including 80 working-class students, school personnel, and community members. They found that working-class Irish students were also very concerned about finances and had fewer resources with which they could purchase additional educational services, such as language instruction and examination preparation common among higher-class students. In addition, the working-class Irish students faced social and cultural barriers. In Egerton's study (2001), working-class students were more likely than their middle- and upper-class peers to begin college at a later age. However, in the Marks et al. study (2003) of English and Scottish working-class adults, subjects did not view higher education as an institution that welcomed them and did not participate because of that view and because familial responsibilities took priority.

Conclusion

Clearly EEC students experience significant challenges as they advance through the educational system. The issues they face and the efforts that would assist them are strikingly similar across all four definitional groups. The research reviewed here illustrates that the students fail to gain access to the college path as early as eighth grade, when they are less likely to have taken algebra I (Adelman, 2006; Akerhielm et al., 1998). From there the challenges mount because low-SES, low-income, first-generation, and working-class students are less likely than their more advantaged peers to have access to a college preparatory high school curriculum, including honors or advanced placement courses

(Adelman, 2006; Akerhielm et al., 1998; Cabrera and La Nasa, 2000b, 2001; Choy et al., 2000; Lynch and O'Riordan, 1998; Martin et al., 2005). The EEC students also form aspirations that are lower than those of their peers (Akerhielm et al., 1998; Terenzini et al., 2001); are less likely to graduate from high school (Bedsworth et al., 2006; Cabrera and La Nasa, 2000b, 2001); have less information available to them about college, the application process, and financial aid (Bedsworth et al., 2006; McDonough, 1997; Walpole et al., 2005); and report high levels of financial concerns associated with college enrollment (Akerhielm et al., 1998; Bedsworth et al., 2006; Connor, 2001; Lynch and O'Riordan, 1998; Paulsen and St. John, 2002; Terenzini et al., 2001).

Finally, EEC students are less likely to enroll in college (Bedsworth et al., 2006; Cabrera and La Nasa, 2000b, 2001; DesJardins et al., 2006; Egerton and Halsey, 1993; Perna and Titus, 2004), enroll in two-year colleges more often than students who come from a more advantaged background (Nunez and Curraco-Alamin, 1998; Perna and Titus, 2004; Rouse, 1994), and are more likely to delay their enrollment (Egerton, 2001; Goldrick-Rab and Han, 2006; Rowan, 2006). The differences are quite stark, with Bedsworth and colleagues (2006) finding that 60 percent of low-income students graduate from high school, 33 percent enter college, and less than 15 percent obtain a bachelor's degree. Cabrera and La Nasa (2000b, 2001) report that less than 15 percent of low-SES students enroll in a four-year college or university and Perna and Titus (2004) report that almost half of low-SES students do not attend a college of any kind.

Several key issues may increase students' access to college, including increasing academic preparation, particularly in math, and increasing access to honors and advanced placement courses (Adelman, 2006; Akerhielm et al., 1998; Cabrera and La Nasa, 2000b, 2001; Choy et al., 2000; Lynch and O'Riordan, 1998; Martin et al., 2005). Raising levels of parental involvement (Bedsworth et al., 2006; Cabrera and La Nasa, 2000b, 2001; Gandara, 1995; Hamrick and Stage, 2004; McCarron and Inkelas, 2006; Perna, 2000b; Terenzini et al., 2001) and creating a supportive environment with school personnel, peer groups, and other mentors available to students (Bedsworth et al., 2006; Gibbons and Shoffner, 2004; Levine and Nidiffer, 1996; McDonough, 1997) also smoothes EEC students' college transitions. Finally, providing aid, and information on aid, is critical (Akerhielm et al., 1998; Bedsworth et al., 2006;

Connor, 2001; DesJardins et al., 2006; Lynch and O'Riordan, 1998; Paulsen and St. John, 2002; Perna and Titus, 2004; Terenzini et al., 2001). The solutions are common across all four definitions of EEC students according to the research findings. So low-SES, low-income, first-generation, and working-class students would all benefit from increased academic preparation, higher parental involvement, a supportive environment, and financial aid and information. These solutions would help every group of EEC students meet the challenges they face in accessing a postsecondary education.

Moreover, the concepts of structure and agency clearly resonate throughout the studies and across the definitions and often provide explanations for the studies' findings. Among the structural challenges that EEC students face are difficulty accessing academically rigorous course work (Adelman, 2006; Akerhielm et al., 1998; Cabrera and La Nasa, 2000b, Terenzini et al., 2001), lack of information about colleges, and lack of financial aid and strategies for accessing the available aid (Akerhielm et al., 1998; Bedsworth et al., 2006; Connor, 2001; DesJardins et al., 2006; Lynch and O'Riordan, 1998; McDonough, 1997; Paulsen and St. John, 2002; Perna and Titus, 2004; Terenzini et al., 2001; Walpole et al., 2005). The ways that agency shapes students' access and enrollment in college are also obvious. Students make decisions that they are comfortable with for a variety of reasons, including their subjective assessments of their ability (McDonough, 1997), the costs of college and available aid (Paulsen and St. John, 2002), and their assessment of psychic costs (Archer and Hutchings, 2000).

Despite the obstacles, there are EEC students who attend college after graduating from high school, and their experiences while there have an effect on their aspirations and eventual attainment. Once again, though, these students face tremendous challenges. We next look at the unique college experiences of EEC students, again reviewing and discussing the literature on low-SES, low-income, first-generation, and working-class students separately.

College Experiences

EXPERIENCES IN COLLEGE HAVE BEEN FOUND TO INFLUENCE students' aspirations and persistence (Astin, 1984, 1993; Tinto, 1987, 1993; Pascarella and Terenzini, 1991, 2005). Astin's theory of involvement (1984, 1993) posits that higher levels of involvement in the campus community, including academic involvement, faculty and student involvement, and students' involvement with other students, result in greater intellectual and social engagement, especially when combined with living on campus, and in higher levels of persistence, aspirations, and attainment.

Social and academic integration are the cornerstones of Tinto's work on persistence (1987, 1993). According to Tinto's model, persistence and eventual attainment are increased when a student is socially and academically integrated into the campus community, strengthening both the institutional fit and the student's commitment to the institution. Many of the studies looked at here note the importance of involvement and integration on students' experiences. In highlighting the differences in college experiences for EEC students, the negative implications for persistence and for students' postcollege opportunities become clear. The difference in college experiences is an area of research on EEC students that has received little attention and therefore is the area in which the greatest opportunity for new research exists.

Socioeconomic Status

Several studies found that differences exist between low- and high-SES students within college academic and cocurricular experiences (Goyette and Mullen, 2006; Terenzini et al., 2001; Titus, 2006c; Walpole, 2003). For example, low-SES students work more and participate less in organized student groups than do their higher-SES peers (Terenzini et al., 2001; Titus, 2006c; Walpole, 2003). Terenzini and colleagues found few academic differences between low- and high-SES students, with the exception that high-SES students are more actively involved in course work than their low-SES counterparts are. Walpole used longitudinal CIRP data collected over a nine-year time line and found that although all students reported spending time with faculty outside class, low-SES students reported spending time with faculty in more structured settings, such as working on a research project, while high-SES students were more likely to report visiting faculty in their homes. Walpole also noted that low-SES students studied less, and both Walpole and Titus showed that these students had lower grade point averages (GPAs) than high-SES students.

In addition, researchers have noted differences in when low- and high-SES students declare a major and in the types of majors they declare. According to Titus (2006c), low-SES students were less likely to have declared a major by the end of their freshman year than were their high-SES peers, and Goyette and Mullen (2006) identified differences in the type of majors low- and high-SES students declared. These researchers used two national databases, NELS 92/94 and Baccalaureate and Beyond (BandB), in addition to information from a *U.S. News and World Report* survey in descriptive and multivariate analyses within a Bourdieuian framework. They concluded that low-SES students were more likely to choose a vocational major such as education or business, while high-SES students were more likely to choose a liberal arts discipline as a major, including math and science, humanities, and social science majors. Goyette and Mullin believe these differences have clear implications for students' future employment and graduate school attendance.

Williams et al. (2005) replicated Davies and Guppy's (1997) work on college students' choices of major with a sample of first-year students from the Survey of Beginning Postsecondary Students (BPS), as opposed to Davies and Guppy's retrospective sample of adults from the NLSY. Williams and colleagues had similar results, however, finding that high-SES students were more likely to choose college majors with lower postcollege incomes than were low-SES students. Furthermore, despite including parental occupation in the SES composite variable, they found that mother's and father's occupational status had an additional and independent effect on the choice of college major. The effect of mother's occupational status was in the same direction as that of SES, while the effect of father's occupational status was in the opposite direction, a finding the authors could not explain. Finally, Trusty, Robinson, Plata, and Ng (2000) found that although SES affected students' choices of majors, gender was a stronger influence. These researchers used NELS : 88 data in a segmentation analysis to model different major choices, which revealed the differing strength of gender versus SES.

Parental Income

In contrast to Titus (2006c) and Walpole (2003), Paulsen and St. John (2002) found that low-income students earned higher grades than their higher-income peers. This may be due in part to the fact that almost half of Paulsen and St. John's low-income students were not traditionally aged students. In addition, almost 20 percent of the low-income students had mothers who had a bachelor's degree or higher. Thus, the low-income population in their sample may have included returning students who were highly motivated and focused on the academic rigors of college. Moreover, according to Paulsen and St. John, low-income students were less likely to live on campus than high-income peers. However, similar to the research on low-SES students, low-income students work more and are less involved in extracurricular activities than their peers from higher-income families (Paulsen and St. John, 2002).

Arzy, Davies, and Harbour (2006) also found that the fourteen low-income students in their phenomenological study maintained low levels of social and cocurricular involvement in order to focus on their academics. They attributed their cautious social and cocurricular involvement to their lack of comfort with their peers and the campus environment. Similarly, they interacted little with faculty inside or outside the classroom, although they did not see this as interfering with their academic focus.

Parental Education

In work on first-generation students' experiences, several studies have found that first-generation students were less academically and socially involved than their non–first-generation peers (Nunez and Cuccaro-Alamin, 1998; Pascarella et al., 2004; Pike and Kuh, 2005; Terenzini, Springer, Yaeger, Pascarella, and Nora, 1996). Specifically, first-generation students were less likely to live on campus or to have favorable perceptions of campus; these students also completed fewer credit hours, worked more, and had lower grades than their peers (Pascarella et al., 2004; Pike and Kuh, 2005; Terenzini et al., 1996). Dennis and colleagues (2005) investigated predictors of first-generation students' GPA, college adjustment, and college commitment. They found that background variables did not predict either adjustment or commitment, and only high school GPA was associated with college GPA. Peer support and motivational factors were other significant predictors. Yet first-generation and low-income students may benefit disproportionately from engaging in classroom activities or collaborative activities and from faculty interaction (Filkins and Doyle, 2002; Pascarella et al., 2004).

Several scholars (Lara, 1992; London, 1992; Rendon, 1992) have written about the cultural dislocation first-generation students experience in college. Rendon and Lara both described the painful processes they went through as students in college because they felt that they had to give up parts of their cultures of origin in order to succeed. Rendon recommended that colleges and universities begin to change their organizational structures in order to accommodate students from nonmajority cultural backgrounds. Such changes are discussed later in the volume.

Parental Occupation

Working-class students' college experiences have been the focus of several essays and opinion pieces. Based on her experiences as a professor, Casey (2005) believed that working-class students had less verbal acuity, were less inclined to join class discussions, and often experienced severe social dislocation. Littrell (1999) reported that working-class students were too often shunted into vocationally oriented majors and needed more courses in the liberal arts in order to promote true social mobility rather than credentialing. O'Dair (2003) agreed with Littrell, particularly viewing working-class students' experiences as socially dislocating because of the hegemonic, bourgeois culture that college campuses perpetuated. These three authors did not explicitly define working class in their essays, and Casey used the term *first generation* alternately with the term *working class.*

Little research exists on working-class students' experiences. The self-identified working-class students in Tett's study (2004), conducted at an elite Scottish university, were also classified as working class by the registrar and were the first in their families to attend university. These students saw both costs and benefits associated with attending university and voiced their feelings of social dislocation in interviews. In results on differences in students' college major by social class, Goldstein (1974) found that intended majors of working-class and upper-class freshmen differed but found no such difference for seniors.

Conclusion

Undoubtedly more research is needed in the area of college experiences for EEC students. From the studies examined here, patterns across all four definitional categories are clear despite the scant number of investigations. Clearly these students are less involved in and integrated into their campuses than their more advantaged peers (Arzy et al., 2006; Nunez and Cuccaro-Alamin, 1998; Pascarella et al., 2004; Paulsen and St. John, 2002; Pike and Kuh, 2005; Terenzini et al., 1996, 2001; Titus, 2006c; Walpole, 2003); in part, this may be related to the fact that they report feeling uncomfortable with peers and in campus activities (Arzy et al., 2006; Lara, 1992; Rendon, 1992; Tett, 2004). The possible effects of students' comfort levels signal the presence of agency in the research on students' experiences. Students decide to become involved based on their comfort levels.

Furthermore, students may be less involved because they work more than their peers do (Pascarella et al., 2004; Paulsen and St. John, 2002; Pike and Kuh, 2005; Terenzini et al., 2001; Terenzini et al., 1996; Titus, 2006c; Walpole, 2003), illustrating a structural factor. Several studies found differences in the types of majors students selected (Davies and Guppy, 1997; Goyette and Mullen, 2006; Trusty et al., 2000; Williams et al., 2005). A student's major is simultaneously a choice, explicatory of agency, and a structuring mechanism. So although structure and agency are conceptually distinct, empirical settings may provide less analytical clarity. The choice of major, as Goyette and Mullen (2006) so clearly indicated, has profound implications for students' outcomes, to which we now turn.

College Outcomes

IN PART BECAUSE OF THEIR DIFFERENT EXPERIENCES ONCE enrolled, EEC students are less likely to persist, graduate from college, or attend graduate school, and they earn lower incomes even when they have attended graduate school than their less challenged peers (Carter, 1999; Horn, 2006; Ishitani, 2006; Nunez and Curraro-Alamin, 1998; Terenzini et al., 2001; Walpole, 2003). In addition, a student's economic and educational background has a direct influence on career aspirations (Smart and Pascarella, 1986; Useem and Karabel, 1990). Since college attendance and graduation are seen as crucial for social mobility and since differential outcomes reduce the possibility for upward mobility, we review the research literature on these EEC student outcomes: persistence, attainment, aspirations, learning outcomes, as well as graduate school attendance, income, and occupational status.

The number of studies focused on each of the outcomes varies widely. Persistence and attainment, for example, have substantial research bases; educational aspirations, learning outcomes, and career orientations are less well documented. This topic of outcomes is organized primarily by the different types of outcomes. Within the section on each particular outcome, I have grouped the studies that use similar definitions if there are sufficient numbers of such studies to justify such a subcategory. For example, the research on persistence and attainment is substantial, so I provide subcategories for socioeconomic status, parental income, parental education, and parental occupation. In contrast, the research in the area of educational aspirations is underdeveloped, so I present all of the findings on this topic without subcategories.

Persistence and Attainment

Because persistence is the first step toward graduation, it is an outcome that mediates other outcomes: attainment, graduate school attendance, income, and career status. EEC students are less likely to persist and less likely to complete college than are their less challenged peers (Gladieux and Swail, 1998; Swail, Cabrera and Lee, 2004; Terenzini et al., 2001; Tinto, 2006; Titus, 2006a, 2006c). Indeed, Tinto (2006) believes understanding that the persistence of EEC students as opposed to more advantaged students is one of the most pressing needs in persistence research.

Socioeconomic Status

In Terenzini et al.'s work (2001), low-SES students were much less likely to finish college than their high-SES peers and were less likely to finish in four years. Anderson and Hearn (1992) similarly concluded that low-SES students' educational attainment was lower than their higher-SES peers when controlling for ability and prior achievement, and that low-SES students were less likely to attend the highly selective institutions that promote persistence and graduation. Walpole (2003) found that low-SES students had lower educational attainments and were less likely to have attended graduate school than their high-SES peers nine years after entering college.

In a study of students' persistence in science, engineering, and mathematics majors, Fenske, Porter, and DuBrock (2000) concluded that needy students, defined as those who either did not receive aid or received aid but still had an unmet need, had higher attrition rates across five years of the study than students who received aid and did not have unmet need. Although he found that SES was not related to students' persistence in the third year of college after controlling for institutional-level financial variables (Titus, 2006d), Titus (2006a, 2006c) said that a higher SES increased the odds of a student's completing college. Then focusing on the role of family wealth in college completion, Titus (2006b) concluded that students from low-wealth families were less likely to complete college in six years than were students from high-wealth families, even after controlling for parental educational and income levels.

Parental Income

In a report documenting the effects of both selectivity and the proportion of low-income students enrolled, Horn (2006) noted that more selective institutions and institutions with smaller cohorts of low-income students had higher graduation rates. She employed Integrated Postsecondary Education Data System (IPEDS) data along with data from the Beginning Postsecondary Students Longitudinal Study (BPS: 96/01). According to the research report, as selectivity declined, the proportion of low-income students grew, and the six-year graduation rates fell. Moreover, at low-income-serving institutions, which she defined as institutions that have 25 percent or more of their students who are Pell grant eligible, those with relatively high graduation rates tended to be private, secular, with large undergraduate populations, and lower enrollments of students of color. Accounting for the reasons for the higher graduation rates was not part of the report's focus, setting the stage for further work.

Several authors (Cabrera et al., 1992; Hwang 2003; Paulsen and St. John, 1997, 2002; St. John et al., 2000) focused on connecting low-income students' persistence to financial aid using the financial nexus model. That model views low-income students' persistence as a complex combination of financial and background variables (Paulsen and St. John, 2002; St. John et al., 2000). Cabrera et al. (1992) found that financial aid had an indirect effect on persistence. Paulsen and St. John (2002) showed that overall, low- and lower-middle-income students were less likely to persist, and middle- and upper-income students were more likely to persist if they were cost conscious when choosing a college. In addition, low-income students' attrition increased when tuition increased. Receiving financial aid further increased low-income students' attrition, a finding the authors believe is due to the inadequacy of financial aid packages for these students.

Parental Education

Also using the financial nexus model, Hwang (2003) focused on first-time, full-time students and found that their persistence depended on living expenses, tuition costs, and the type of institution they attended. Students whose mothers had degrees from community colleges were less likely to persist at public colleges and universities. In contrast, having a mother with a bachelor degree or higher increased students' likelihood of persistence at public institutions compared to students whose mothers had a high school diploma or less. However, at private colleges, this relationship changed, and students with more highly educated mothers were less likely to persist than students whose mothers did not attend college.

Several authors have investigated the persistence behavior of first-generation students. Ishitani (2006) and Nunez and Curraro-Alamin (1998) found that first-generation students persist at lower levels than their non-first-generation peers. Ishitani (2006) used NELS:88 data with transcript information and survival analysis and concluded that persistence increased with each increment of parental education, with students with two college-educated parents being the most likely to persist. Also, although first-generation students left college in high numbers in their first year, the second year was when the highest amount of attrition occurred for students whose parents did not have education beyond high school. Furthermore, after Ishitani controlled for other background variables, he reported that in the first year of college, students from the lowest income category were more likely to leave than students from higher-income categories. After controlling for several additional demographic and institutional level variables, Nunez and Curraro-Alamin (1998) reported that first-generation students' persistence was lower at both two- and four-year institutions than their non-first-generation peers.

Nunez and Curraro-Alamin (1998) employed the Beginning Postsecondary Longitudinal Study (BPS: 90/94) and Baccalaureate and Beyond Longitudinal Study (BandB: 93/94) to examine attainment for first-generation students. Of the first-generation students they studied who started full time in 1989–1990, almost 20 percent had obtained a bachelor's degree by 1994, compared to 38 percent of students whose parents had above a high school diploma and 43 percent of students whose parents had a bachelor's degree or advanced degree. McCarron and Inkelas (2006) also focused on degree attainment for first-generation students using NELS:88/2000 data, which examines a longer time frame than the BPS data. Their analysis showed that over 60 percent of first-generation students did not attain the degree to which they had aspired in 1990. Moreover, less than 30 percent of the students had completed a bachelor's degree, compared to 56 percent of the students who were not first generation. A substantial majority of the students who had aspired to a four-year degree but had not attained it by 2000 did attempt some postsecondary education; however, either they did not finish, obtained a certificate, or obtained an associate degree instead. Ishitani (2006) found that compared to students whose parents had graduated from college, first-generation students were half as likely to graduate in four years and a third less likely to do so in five years.

Educational Aspirations

In unpublished studies, Boatsman (1995) and Hoffnung and Sack (1981) noted that the educational aspirations of low-SES college students are lower than those of high-SES college students. However, neither of these studies employed adequate controls to isolate the effects of SES and college impact. Boatsman's findings (1995), however, support the importance of both involvement and faculty contact in positively influencing aspirations. Variables that were significant in predicting increased aspirations during college included being president of a student organization, spending time with faculty outside class, and visiting a professor's home. Other research (Walpole, 2003), however, has identified low-SES students as less likely to participate in student clubs and organizations or to visit faculty in their homes than were their high-SES peers. Possible reasons for the differences include that low-SES students were working more hours. These results suggest that low-SES students have fewer environmentally linked inducements that raise aspirations or attainment than their high-SES peers.

Moreover, Walpole (2003) found that low-SES students were less likely to aspire to a law or medical degree and more likely to aspire to a master's degree than were their high-SES peers. Segal, DeMeis, Wood, and Smith (2001) wrote that low-SES students were less likely to expect to finish college or earn a graduate degree than were high-SES students. Similarly, first-generation students' aspirations and plans for educational attainment were lower than those of non-first-generation students (Pascarella et al., 2004; Pike and Kuh, 2005). In addition, low-income students had lower educational aspirations than higher-income students (Paulsen and St. John, 2002). However, Goldstein

(1974) found no differences in the educational aspirations of working-class versus upper-middle-class students in his study of students at Brown University, which may be due to the selective nature of his sample and the more historical nature of his study. Study authors posit that financial factors, including the need to pay off undergraduate loans prior to graduate school, and lower grades may shape these students' aspirations (Paulsen and St. John, 2002; Walpole, 2003).

Learning Outcomes

Students attend college to gain knowledge and skills for obtaining employment and for graduate school admission, so identifying differences in learning outcomes is important. Terenzini et al. (2001) examined several learning outcomes and reported generally similar findings for low- and high-SES students. Several studies of learning outcomes in first-generation students, however, had mixed results. In one study, Terenzini and colleagues (1996) employed National Study of Students Learning (NSSL) data, a longitudinal database with eighteen participating institutions, and found with regression techniques that despite lower initial academic achievement in math, reading, and critical thinking, first-generation students experienced similar cognitive gains as traditional students in first-year critical thinking and mathematics, while traditional students reported higher first-year increases in reading skills than first-generation students. Pascarella et al. (2004) used NSSL data too, but examined three-year outcomes in learning. In their regression analyses, only small and nonsignificant differences showed up in first-generation students' cognitive outcomes as compared to non-first-generation students. In a third study focused on first-generation students, Pike and Kuh (2005) employed data from the College Students Experiences Questionnaire (CSEQ) and structural equation modeling. In contrast to the previous two studies, first-generation students reported lower levels of intellectual development than their non-first-generation peers, which may have been a result of their higher rates of living off campus. Clearly, given the importance of understanding the extent of students' learning, further work in this area is necessary, particularly given the mixed results.

Graduate School Attendance, Income, and Occupational Status

Students' aspirations are critical to eventual attainment and subsequently to other outcomes as well, including income and careers. Research into the differential effect of college on EEC students has revealed mixed and inconsistent data on income and occupational status (Anderson and Hearn, 1992; Bowles and Gintis, 1976, 2002; Egerton, 2001; Goldstein, 1974; Goyette and Mullen, 2006; Jencks et al., 1979; Katchadourian and Boli, 1994; Perna, 2005; Terenzini et al., 2001; Walpole, 2003; Wachtel, 1975; Zweigenhaft, 1993). This section highlights that research. There is substantial research in this area using SES but much less using the other three definitions. Accordingly, studies using SES are reviewed in the next section as a group, and all other definitions are combined and reviewed following the SES section.

Socioeconomic Status

In several studies (Goyette and Mullen, 2006; Terenzini et al., 2001; Walpole, 2003), low-SES students were less likely to attend graduate school than were high-SES students. Overall, using CIRP data, Smart and Pascarella (1986) found that initial SES directly affected the subsequent SES for White females and had a significant, but indirect, effect for White males and minority females. Originating SES had no effect on subsequent SES for minority males. In addition to SES, the other demographic variables that played a role in subsequent SES were students' initial career aspirations and high school academic achievement.

Walpole (2003) found that low-SES students reported lower incomes, even when working full time and after attending graduate school. Furthermore, different experiences in college predicted graduate school attendance for low- and high-SES students in the logistic regression analyses. Working on a professor's research project, time spent talking to faculty outside class, participating in intercollegiate sports, and college GPA significantly increased the likelihood that low-SES students would attend graduate school, while only GPA significantly increased the chances that a high-SES student would attend graduate school. Similarly, Wachtel (1975), as well as Bowles and Gintis (1976, 2002), found that college graduates from higher SES backgrounds have higher incomes and overall socioeconomic statuses than those from lower SES backgrounds. Moreover, Bowles and Gintis (2002), using a series of production functions and correlations, demonstrated that family wealth had the strongest link to intergenerational status. Finally, Anderson and Hearn (1992) concluded that higher socioeconomic status is associated with higher occupational status and higher income after completing college. The findings regarding differential outcomes for students from high-SES backgrounds were contradicted by several authors, including Jencks and colleagues (1979), whose found work with several different samples identified no such differences.

According to Goyette and Mullen (2006), students majoring in vocational fields, who disproportionately were from low-SES backgrounds, were more likely to be employed full time five years after graduation than students who majored in traditional liberal arts fields, who were disproportionately from high-SES families. Students with majors in vocational fields were also earning slightly more than liberal arts majors after graduation. The exact opposite pattern prevailed with graduate school enrollment: liberal arts majors were more likely than vocational majors to have enrolled in graduate school in the same time frame. These authors believed that the results pointed to a two-track system in higher education: one for low-SES and one for high-SES students. They reported that the disproportionate graduate school attendance by liberal arts majors, who tended to be higher SES, positioned those students in the long term for higher-status, higher-paying positions than students majoring in vocational fields.

Following a class from Stanford University for a decade after graduation, Katchadourian and Boli (1994) found evidence of intergenerational mobility for students from low-SES backgrounds but also noted that these students had not attained socioeconomic statuses as high as their peers from high-SES origins. In another study involving relative social class standing, Zweigenhaft (1993) investigated the educational attainment of Harvard graduates and concluded that students from public high schools who graduated from Harvard were more likely to receive doctoral degrees than were Harvard graduates who had attended elite boarding schools. In contrast, elite boarding school graduates were more likely to receive law and business management degrees. According to the author, the boarding school graduates were more likely to originate in upper-class families and have lower test scores and high school grades than the public school graduates, but SES and ability were not control measures in the study. Additional research (Useem and Karabel, 1990) on the economic outcomes of graduates of highly selective colleges and universities indicated that those from low-SES backgrounds may not reach top corporate positions in proportion to their population.

Parental Income, Education, and Occupation

Perna (2005) reported that graduates from the second income quartile (the second lowest) experienced a smaller gain in earnings from receiving a college degree than the other quartiles. Her findings also showed that individuals from the highest income quartile with a bachelor's degree reported the highest earnings of all quartiles.

In examining outcomes for first-generation students, Nunez and Cuccaro-Alamin (1998) saw no differences in employment rates between first-generation students who received a certificate or degree and their non-first-generation peers. Moreover, first-generation students were more likely to be employed in a field related to their education than were their peers. First-generation students who held bachelor's degrees also reported similar incomes as their non-first-generation peers.

In a study of the social backgrounds of high achievers, Youn, Arnold, and Salkever (1999) examined the career achievements of American Rhodes scholars from the 1940s and 1960s. They found few differences in scholars' social origins in the two samples; the vast majority came from middle- and upper-middle-class backgrounds, with less than 10 percent reporting skilled, semi-skilled, or unskilled manual labor occupations for their fathers. Furthermore, the scholars were successful in their careers; 32 percent appeared in *Who's Who* because of their achievements, and several were nationally prominent leaders. Social origins were not associated with appearing in *Who's Who*.

Goldstein (1974) noted no significant differences in his study at Brown University between working-class and upper-middle-class students' plans following graduation. Egerton (2001) found that working-class students who began college at a later age than their more advantaged peers had similar experiences in the job market as their peers following graduation. In other words, college was providing an avenue of social mobility for the students in her study.

Career Orientation

Perhaps the different majors of low- versus high-SES students (Goyette and Mullen, 2006) and the higher incomes found for students from high-SES backgrounds (Walpole, 2003) are due to different career aspirations. In focusing on differences in career choices, Farmer (1978) suggested that students from low-SES backgrounds saw less explicit connections between education and particular careers than did high-SES students; rather, low-SES students had a vague belief that higher education brought less economic hardship, but no specific understandings of the range of career options and connections between education and specific careers. Similarly, Gibbons and Shoffner (2004), using a case study design, illustrated the necessity of a multistep process to assist first-generation students in understanding the links among high school curricular choices, higher education enrollment, and career paths. Stitt-Gohdes (1997) suggested that traditional developmental theories needed to be modified to address low-income students. She particularly believed that low-income students incorporated economic realities and their perceptions of the choices available to them in career decisions and that counselors needed to address these issues in counseling these students. Slaney and Brown (1983) found that low-SES students indicated higher preferences for realistic careers as measured by the Vocational Preference Inventory than did high-SES students. In addition, low-SES students indicated clearer choices of college majors and lower levels of career indecision than did high-SES students. These scholars were contradicted by Luzzo (1992), who saw no differences in career development among students from different social class backgrounds.

Conclusion

Clearly the research in the area of students' outcomes is mixed. Knowledge in the areas of educational aspirations, learning outcomes, and career orientations is noticeably scant; research on persistence, attainment, graduate school attendance, income, and occupation status is more substantial although uneven in focus. Overall, the studies illustrate the continuing trials that EEC students face. Despite their successful negotiation of the impediments encountered in enrolling in college, they are less likely to persist once they enroll and less likely to obtain a bachelor's degree than their peers. It also seems clear that low-SES students are less likely to attend graduate school than their high-SES peers, and aspire to and obtain different types of graduate degrees, but research is needed on such attendance for low-income, first-generation, and working-class students to gain insight into the extent to which these other groups within the EEC umbrella have similar outcomes. There are many possible reasons for this, including the different types of institutions attended (Anderson and Hearn, 1992; Horn, 2006) and different majors chosen (Goyette and Mullen, 2006). Once again, both structural factors and agency noticeably shape the findings in this area. The structural factor that was most apparent was the financial factor (Cabrera et al., 1992; Fenske et al., 2000; Paulsen and St. John, 1997, 2002; St. John et al., 2000; Titus, 2006a, 2006b, 2006c). The type of institution attended and major field in college structure students' outcomes, yet there is a measure of student choice, or agency, in both, again highlighting the blurring that can occur between structure and agency in empirical settings.

In addition to the need for more research and information in the area of outcomes, additional information on students may assist in understanding not only their outcomes but their access to college and experiences once they enroll. In the United States, social structure clearly poses social class issues, but must also take race, ethnicity, and gender into account in order to understand, and improve, students' access and attainment. We next focus on the multiple identities that shape access to, progress in, and attainment from higher education.

Social Class Effects and Multiple Identities

S TUDENTS FROM DIFFERENT SOCIAL CLASS BACKGROUNDS are a diverse group, and the intersections of class, gender, and racial/ethnic statuses provide heterogeneity in educational achievement and attainment (Davis, 1998; Freeman, 1997, 1999; Nunez et al., 2004; Perna, 2004, 2005; Perna and Titus, 2005; Walpole, in press). In studying this diverse group, researchers have two approaches. The first is to attempt to account for the contribution of each status. This approach can be difficult because disentangling the contribution of each variable is daunting. The other approach is to focus on the overlapping nature of the statuses and the synergy with which they contribute to students' experiences and outcomes. With either approach, it is critical to understand how the intersections of students' social class, gender, and racial/ethnic identities shape issues of access and admission, as well as college experiences and outcomes.

Here we review the literature on these status intersections and illustrate the saliency of understanding students from these multiple vantage points. Although there has appropriately been increasing attention to the effects of race, ethnicity, and gender in higher education, I specifically focus on higher education literature that provides insights into these areas as they intersect with socioeconomic status, income status, first-generation status, and social class status. Although the literature examining each racial, gender, or ethnic group by itself is interesting and informative, my purpose here is to explore the connectedness between those literatures and the literatures on EEC students. The literature reviewed in this section thus focuses on the synergy between EEC students' experiences and outcomes and students from various racial and ethnic groups, as well as on the synergy between EEC students and gender considerations.

Not all racial, ethnic, and gender groups have received equivalent attention in the higher education literature, and not all topics have equally addressed these overlapping class, race, ethnic, and gender statuses. Thus, this material is organized around two topics: college access and choice, and college experiences and outcomes. In these sections, similar studies are grouped together.

College Access and Choice

Several studies have focused on multiple identities in the college choice process. Hamrick and Stage (2004) used NELS data to construct causal models of college predispositions for White, African American, and Latino and Latina students at high schools with predominantly low-income students. The models were constructed explicitly to try to account for the effects of community activities and mentors on students' predispositions to college, and parental education and family income were separate variables rather than being combined into a composite. For White students, parental expectations were the strongest direct predictor for students' predisposition to college. Parental education, family income, being a female student, and having high levels of community involvement had significant positive effects on parents' expectations. Parents' education also significantly affected students' grades and community activities, and family income was significantly related to grades.

Family income also directly affected parents' expectations for African American students, and both parental education and family income significantly affected students' grades, while parental education directly and significantly affected African American students' predispositions (Hamrick and Stage, 2004). Higher levels of parental education were also significantly related to Latinas' college predisposition and to parental expectations, while family income was directly related to parental expectations and community activities. Community activities were significantly associated with parental expectations and students' grades. For Latinos, the model predictions were quite different from those for other students because there were only two significant associations: family income was directly associated with college predispositions, and parents' education was significantly related to parental expectations. Although the models for each group incorporated community activities and mentors, neither directly affected any of the students' predispositions to college.

McDonough and Antonio (1996) employed CIRP data and found that measures of SES were associated with higher selectivity in White students' college choices but not African American, Latino, or Asian American students' choices. Beattie (2002) found that although low-SES White male students' college enrollment patterns fit with human capital theory, enrollment patterns of high-SES, women students, and African American students were not associated with the economic returns of enrollment.

DesJardins et al. (2006) reported that low-income students were less likely to enroll in college than high-income students across all racial and ethnic groups, although high-income African Americans were less likely to enroll than high-income Whites or Asian Americans. Hurtado, Inkelas, Briggs, and Rhee (1997) used NELS:88/92 and BPS:90/92 data to investigate college choice experiences among several groups of students and found that low-income White and Latino students submitted the fewest college applications and that the number of applications increased as income increased. Asian American students submitted similar numbers of applications across all income groups, and only the lowest-income African American students applied to fewer institutions than other African American income groups. Parents' education level was a significant predictor of the number of applications submitted only for White students.

Employing NELS:88/94 data and a modified human capital theory framework, Perna (2000a) noted that a higher parental education level increased the probability that African American and White students would attend four-year institutions after high school, but it did not affect Latino students' chances. Alternatively, higher family income increased Latino students' probability of attending four-year institutions. Furthermore, her research demonstrated that African American students were more likely than White or Latino students to attend four-year institutions, although receiving loans as part of a financial aid package reduced African Americans' likelihood of attending a four-year college. African American women and White women were more likely than

African American and White men to enroll in four-year institutions after high school, and White women were more likely than White men to attend a community college (Perna, 2000b).

Several authors have focused on the college choice process for African American students. Horvat (1996a, 1996b, 1997, 2003) and Horvat and Antonio (1999) explored the intersection of race and class in their studies of African American girls' college choice processes using a Bourdieuian framework. The qualitative studies found that students' race, social class, and the organizational structure of their high schools shaped the students' college choice processes. Horvat found that African American students attending the low-SES and mixed-SES schools had more constrained college choice sets than students, regardless of social class background, who attended the highly selective private girls high school. The girls attending the two public schools applied more often to public universities within their state, while the girls attending the private high school applied predominantly to private universities in other states. McDonough et al. (1997) found that African American students who attended Historically Black Colleges and Universities (HBCUs) had mothers with higher levels of education than all students, as well as higher than African American students who attended Predominantly White Institutions (PWIs). Having a mother with a higher level of education also increased the odds of an African American student's attending an HBCU in the logistic regression analysis. McDonough et al. (1997) employed CIRP data and a Bourdieuian framework.

Several studies have confirmed that African American students were less likely to attend their first-choice institutions than all students or White students (Carter, 1999; Hurtado et al., 1997; McDonough et al., 1997). In Carter's study (1999), African American students' lower SES compared to White students explained much of the differences in college choice between the two groups. African American students were more likely than White students to attend institutions closer to home, public institutions, and colleges and universities that cost less. Both African American and White students' degree aspirations were associated with mother's education.

Freeman (1997) investigated African American college choice and found that students perceived many obstacles, including costs. Furthermore, students' perceptions of obstacles to attending college often hindered their participation.

Nettles and Perna (1997) found that African American students seeking bachelor's degrees had higher SES and parents who had higher incomes and more education than students beginning at community colleges. Moreover, African American women who received bachelor's degrees in their sample were more likely to be first-generation students than were the men in the sample.

Terenishi et al. (2004) investigated college choice, ethnicity, and SES among Asian American and Pacific Islanders using CIRP data. They noted that Chinese and Korean Americans were the most likely of the five ethnic subgroups to attend highly selective colleges, Japanese Americans were the most likely to attend private colleges, and Chinese and Japanese Americans were the most likely to attend private universities. Higher percentages of Filipino and Southeast Asian Americans attended public colleges. Low-income Chinese and Korean Americans (those with families earning less than $25,000) were the most likely to attend highly selective institutions, while low-income Southeast Asian and Filipino Americans were most likely to attend public colleges. High-income Filipino and Japanese Americans (those with families earning more than $75,000) attended low-selectivity colleges and universities in high percentages (75 percent and 68 percent, respectively). Filipino and Southeast Asian Americans were the most likely of all the ethnic groups to choose a college because they wanted to be close to home, to report that they had major financial concerns, and to apply to only one institution. Chinese Americans and Korean Americans reported the highest rates of attending preparation courses for the SATs, consulting national rankings magazines in their college choice, and applying to five or more colleges and universities. Yet low-income Chinese, Korean, and Filipino Americans were most likely to report making their choice of college because of low tuition. In regression analyses, parental income and education levels were significant predictors of attending a more selective institution, as was being Chinese or Korean American.

Also using CIRP data, Nunez, McDonough, Ceja, and Solorzano (2004) explored ethnic differences in Latino students' college choice processes. They reported that Mexican Americans incorporated family and home influences into their college choice more often than did Puerto Ricans and were more likely to attend a Hispanic-serving institution than were Puerto Ricans. Moreover, the Mexican Americans were more likely to have taken Advanced

Placement courses. Chicanos also reported lower levels of parental education than Puerto Ricans. Bohon, Johnson, and Gorman (2006) also investigated ethnic differences among Latino students' college choice processes. In this study, Cuban American high school students had higher aspirations and expectations for college attendance than White students and Puerto Rican and Mexican American high school students. For Puerto Rican and Mexican American students, socioeconomic status explained the lower aspirations and expectations, but were not significantly associated with Cuban Americans' aspirations and expectations. Swail, Cabrera, and Lee (2004) found that Latino students may be particularly disadvantaged in the college choice process because they are disproportionately from low-SES families. Montelongo (2003) noted that Latino students' parental education level was significantly and positively associated with academic achievement.

Two studies examined the effects of multiple identities on college choice in Britain. Ball et al. (2002) investigated ethnic minority students' college choice processes in Britain and found that parents' education played a significant role, with students from families without a college education, who were working class and low income, explicitly choosing to attend university despite the obstacles posed, while students with educated parents assumed they would attend university. Marks et al. (2003) found that working-class women in the United Kingdom did not view higher education as a realistic option in part because of family responsibilities, but that the few women who did pursue higher education reported doing so in order to provide role models for their own children.

Experiences and Outcomes

Few studies have addressed the college experiences and outcomes of students with multiple identities. Walpole (in press) employed longitudinal CIRP data and a Bourdieuian framework and concluded that African American students' college experiences and outcomes vary by SES, with low-SES African American students reporting lower grades, less involvement in the college environment, and more time spent working than their high-SES peers. In addition, low-SES African American students reported lower aspirations for doctoral, law, and medical degrees than their peers from higher-SES families and were less likely to have attended graduate school nine years after beginning college than those peers. Moreover, African American students from low-SES families reported lower incomes than their high-SES peers nine years after beginning college.

Paulsen and St. John (2002) found that among their two lowest-income groups, African Americans persisted at higher rates than White students did. Latino students chose colleges that had lower costs, and they were less likely to take out loans than other racial and ethnic groups. Furthermore, low-income Asian American students were less likely to persist than other groups in their study. Finally, low-income women were less likely to persist than low-income men.

McCarron and Inkelas's study (2006) of first-generation students' degree attainment found that Asian Americans were more likely to have obtained a bachelor's degree: 42 percent had done so by 2000 compared to 31 percent of White students, 21 percent of African American students, and 19 percent of Latino students. They identified no gender differences in degree attainment overall, although SES did show an effect: almost 80 percent of low-SES students did not obtain a four-year degree compared to 48 percent of the highest-SES students. Their SES measure was relative to the sample. Dennis and colleagues' (2005) study of first-generation Latino and Asian American students found that Asian American students had significantly higher high school and college GPAs than Latino students.

According to Perna (2004), parental education was significantly associated with graduate school enrollment across all gender and racial ethnic groups. In this study, she used Baccalaureate and Beyond data (BandB: 93/97) and a modified human capital theoretical frame. Among different racial and ethnic groups, Asian Americans were more likely to enroll in graduate school than were White, African American, or Latino students. Also, women were more likely to pursue graduate education than were men across all racial and ethnic groups. Furthermore, White women, African American women, and Latinas enrolled most often in master's degree programs, while Asian American women enrolled most often in programs lower than master's degree programs. African American men enrolled in master's degree programs most often, and Asian American men enrolled in first professional degree programs most often. White men and Latinos enrolled in programs that provided less than a master's degree.

Several additional studies have addressed gender issues. Perna (2005) found that women who earned a bachelor's degree enjoyed an increase in their average wage compared to women who did not attend college, as did men who attended college compared to men who did not attend college. However, the gap between women who secured a bachelor's degree and women who did not attend college was larger than the gap between men who obtained the degree and men who did not. Perna employed NELS:92/2000 data in her analysis as well as a human capital framework. Allen and Haniff (1991) determined that African American women experienced a more difficult academic transition than men at both HBCUs and PWIs and that African American students at PWIs had lower GPAs than students at HBCUs. In addition, although African American women at PWIs were socially isolated, Fleming (1984) found that these women more fully developed their intellectual skills than did women at HBCUs. She attributed this to their ability to develop what she termed "assertiveness" because there were fewer dominant African American men on the PWI campuses and because it was necessary to be assertive in an environment that these students perceived as hostile.

However, Jackson (1998) noted that African American women at coeducational PWIs focused on their racial identities and did not develop their gender identities as fully. In that study, the coeducational PWIs focused support on African American students and on women students and did not address the unique needs of students who were both. According to Slaney and Brown (1983), low-SES African American male students anticipated interpersonal conflict as possible career obstacles more often than did high-SES African American men. Low-SES White men saw school-related obstacles as potentially limiting their career goals more often than did low-SES African American men.

Additional studies incorporating multiple identities have focused on first-generation students. Rendon (1992), Lara (1992), and Saunders and Serna (2004) all wrote about the struggles that first-generation Latino students faced in negotiating the cultural differences between their home environments and the college choice process and college environments. Rendon and Lara described their own difficulty in maintaining their cultures of origin during the educational process and the pain of feeling caught between the two cultures. Saunders and Serna's study illustrated that the most successful students in negotiating the college choice process were those who could simultaneously maintain old networks and create new ones.

Weis (1992) described the experiences of African American first-generation students in an urban community college as filled with tensions based on social class and gender. The students viewed the mostly middle-class African American faculty with disdain for not behaving in ways the students thought appropriate. The students believed the faculty had achieved success and were uninterested in helping students succeed. The gender tension was within the African American community. Women felt that men were not serious about their studies and not taking enough responsibility for their education. In addition, Kiang (1992) described the difficulties first-generation Asian American students faced because they were assumed to need little assistance. On the contrary, they experienced significant levels of difficulty in adjusting to a new cultural context and often experienced difficulty because English was not their first language.

Conclusion

The importance of accounting for students' multiple identities becomes obvious from this research. EEC students are a heterogeneous group, and in order to understand their educational access, progress, and outcomes, it is critical to take that heterogeneity into account. This is a challenge because researchers already have a diversity of definitions and conceptual approaches and models. Finding ways to account for the complexities of students' lived realities should involve learning from and perhaps combining new conceptual models. In the U.S. context, social structure is complicated by class status as well as race, ethnicity, and gender. In addition, Conley (1999–2000) points to the need to take wealth into account, particularly when examining socioeconomic status within the African American community. For example, Bourdieu's work was done on French social structure and did not account for the demographic diversity and social structures found in the United States (Carter, 2003). Although those social categories act as structuring mechanisms, researchers must be careful to account for both structure and agency, since so many studies have found that they work in concert (McDonough, 1997; Paulsen and St. John, 2000; Walpole, 2003).

The next topic is the multitude of organizational responses, which can also be considered structuring mechanisms shaping students' experiences and outcomes.

Organizational Structures, Practices, and Responses

WHEN EEC STUDENTS ENROLL IN HIGHER EDUCATION organizations, the type of institution they attend clearly shapes their college experiences and subsequent outcomes. For example, some EEC students attend community colleges, some attend highly selective institutions, and many attend public comprehensive universities. Each of these institutions has a different mission, organizational structure, and resource base from which to draw, and these differences shape students, experiences and outcomes. Moreover, some institutions have designed specific programs to assist EEC students in their transition to and participation in postsecondary education. The differences in organizational structure and responses are the focus here.

Low-SES, low-income, first-generation, and working-class students attend different types of institutions from their higher-SES, higher-income, non-first-generation, and more upper-class peers (Anderson and Hearn, 1992; Astin, 1993, 1999; Astin and Oseguera, 2004; Borrego, 2001; Bowen et al., 2005; Carnevale and Rose, 2004; Hearn, 1984, 1990, 1991; Karabel, 2005; Martin et al., 2005; McDonough, 1997; Terenzini et al., 2001; Tinto, 2006; Titus, 2006b, 2006c). EEC students are more likely to attend less selective and public institutions and less likely to attend more selective colleges or universities than other students (Anderson and Hearn, 1992; Astin, 1993, 1999; Astin and Oseguera, 2004; Bowen et al., 2005; Carnevale and Rose, 2004; Hearn, 1984, 1990, 1991; Karabel, 2005; Martin et al., 2005; McDonough, 1997; Terenzini et al., 2001; Tinto, 2006). In fact, in the past thirty years, access to selective institutions has decreased for low-SES students (Astin and Osegura, 2004; Bowen et al., 2005; Carnevale and Rose, 2004; Karabel, 2005; Tinto, 2006).

Higher selectivity, however, is associated with higher persistence and graduation rates (Astin, 1993, 1999; Astin and Osegura, 2004; Bowen et al., 2005; Bowen and Bok, 1998; Carnevale and Rose, 2004; Karabel, 2005; Tinto, 2006; Titus, 2006c) and many think with access to more selective graduate programs and access to high-status career tracks (Carnevale and Rose, 2004; Domhoff, 1983; Katchadourian and Boli, 1994; Useem and Karabel, 1990; Zweigenhaft, 1993). We examine the extent to which particular types of institutions' structures and practices promote differential outcomes for EEC students and explore specific programming responses colleges have had for EEC students that have been successful in promoting their transition, persistence, cognitive gains, engagement, and graduation. In examining these factors, I draw on topics and research that provide insight into organizational structures, practices, and responses that are most directly relevant to EEC students. Although a substantial body of organizational research on higher education institutions has evolved, I do not focus broadly on organizational issues in higher education but rather on issues that affect EEC students.

Organizational Structures and Practices

EEC students disproportionately attend less selective public institutions, especially community colleges (Nunez and Curraco-Alamin, 1998; Perna and Titus, 2004; Rouse, 1994; Terenzini et al., 2001; Titus, 2006c). Community colleges attract low-SES students, both those aspiring to terminal associate degrees and those aspiring to transfer to four-year institutions (Karabel, 1972; Karabel and Astin, 1975; Bowles and Gintis, 1976; Hoffnung and Sack, 1981). Yet attendance at community colleges has been found to have a negative impact on persistence and attainment (Pascarella and Terenzini, 1991, 2005; Terenzini et al., 2001), often through the "cooling-out" function in which counselors steer students toward vocational programs and quick placement in the occupational structure (Clark, 1960). Transfer rates at community colleges are also associated with socioeconomic status, and community colleges that have high proportions of high-SES students also have high transfer rates (Wassmer, Moore, and Shulock, 2004), and socioeconomic status significantly predicts the likelihood that students will transfer (Hagedorn, Lester, Moon, and Tibbetts, 2006).

Scholars in addition believe that community colleges' curricula, management systems, and disciplinary procedures reinforce movement into the lower strata of the occupational hierarchy, limiting student attainment (Bowles and Gintis, 1976; Brint and Karabel, 1989). Hoffnung and Sack (1981) found that the structure of colleges and universities attended by low-SES students direct them toward lower positions in the occupational structure and away from graduate school attendance by discouraging independent thought and problem solving. Littrell (1999) believes that the institutions low-SES students attend, particularly lower-selectivity state universities, focus on vocational education rather than the liberal arts education they were originally entrusted to provide.

Small residential colleges and selective colleges have been found to positively influence aspirations and persistence, but low-SES students are much less likely to attend these institutions (Astin, 1975, 1993, 1999; Astin and Oseguera, 2004; Boatsman, 1995; Carnevale and Rose, 2004). Carter (1999) found that attending a four-year institution was significantly associated with higher degree expectations for both White and African American students. Titus (2006b, 2006c) reported that students who attend private institutions, colleges with larger endowment incomes, and colleges with higher educational and general spending per full-time-equivalent student are more likely to graduate, but low-SES students are less likely than their high-SES peers to attend such institutions. In contrast, students attending institutions with higher percentages of tuition and fees in total revenue are more likely to graduate, and low-SES students are more likely than their high-SES peers to attend these colleges (Titus, 2006c). Anderson and Hearn (1992) concluded that low-SES students were less likely to attend the highly selective institutions that promote persistence and graduation. These colleges are also more likely to foster development of traits compatible with high-status occupational positions and graduate school attendance (Bowles and Gintis, 1976; Hoffnung and Sack, 1981).

Scholars believe that highly selective institutions provide a high-quality undergraduate experience (Astin, 1993, 1999; Kingston and Smart, 1990) and have been linked to high-status occupations and high income (Carnevale and Rose, 2004; Domhoff, 1983; Hoffnung and Sack, 1981; Kingston and Lewis, 1990; Kingston and Smart, 1990; Solmon, 1975; Useem and Karabel, 1980; Youn et al., 1999). Solmon (1975) found college quality was positively related to earnings over a lifetime. Kingston and Smart (1990) agreed that attendance at an elite institution makes a significant difference in income, providing an advantage early in a graduate's career that continues through the peak career years. In addition, graduates of elite undergraduate institutions received an added bonus in high-prestige graduate and professional school applications, which further contributes to outcome measures of income, occupational status, and educational attainments. Scholars have posited that the structure of prestigious institutions encourages leadership, independent learning, and problem-solving skills valued in high-status, high-paying occupations (Bowles and Gintis, 1976; Hoffnung and Sack, 1981).

Bowen and Bok's study (1998) of elite institutions revealed that students not only graduated in higher percentages and went on to attend graduate and professional school in high proportions, they were also more involved with their communities after finishing college. These results were true for both White and African American students and true for both students admitted with and without the assistance of affirmative action. Although lower-SES (based on parental education and family income) students were less likely to graduate than their high-SES peers, their graduation rate was still quite high, at 74 percent. The same was true of their income: high-SES students earned more following college than low-SES students, although low-SES men were earning over $70,000 annually and the women over $55,000 annually. The authors conclude that there is considerable evidence for upward mobility; however, only 1 percent of White students at the institutions in their study originated from low-SES families.

Goldstein's findings (1974) contradict those of Bowen and Bok (1998) regarding differences in outcomes based on SES of origin. His study of Brown University undergraduates uncovered no differences between working-class and upper-middle-class students in college experiences, educational or career aspirations, or expected satisfaction levels with particular careers. He attributed this finding to the selective admissions process in which the working-class students who had most likely engaged in anticipatory socialization were admitted. Furthermore, he believed that given the results, attendance at Brown was furthering the working-class students' upward mobility. The differences between Goldstein's and Bowen and Bok's findings are most likely due to generational differences and the social change that occurred between the time frames of the two studies.

More recently, Dale and Krueger (2002) explored whether college type made a difference or whether it was the characteristics of the students who attended that resulted in higher earnings. They found that students' subsequent earnings are not related to selectivity; rather, the cost of the college is the key variable: students who attended more expensive universities earned more money following college than did students of similar ability who attended less costly institutions. Moreover, they found that low-SES students enjoyed a greater earnings boost from attending an expensive college than their more advantaged peers did.

Goldstein's (1974) and Dale and Kruger's (2002) findings notwithstanding, many scholars believe that elite institutions provide a differential benefit to their alumni (Carnevale and Rose, 2004; Domhoff, 1983; Hoffnung and Sack, 1981; Kingston and Lewis, 1990; Kingston and Smart, 1990; Martin et al., 2005; Solmon, 1975; Useem and Karabel, 1990; Youn et al., 1999). Perhaps part of the advantage of an elite education in the marketplace results from the academic preparation and undergraduate experience at these institutions. Many of these institutions are small liberal arts institutions, most have high endowments, and they offer an undergraduate experience built on years of tradition and success in placing graduates (Astin, 1999; Kingston and Lewis, 1990). The majority of these institutions are residential, have low faculty-to-student ratios that afford more opportunities for faculty and student involvement, and offer a wide variety of cocurricular opportunities (Astin, 1993; Hoffnung and Sack, 1981; Kingston and Lewis, 1990). These are some of the environmental factors that produce the greatest change in students during college and have a positive effect on aspirations and persistence (Astin, 1985, 1993, 1999; Boatsman, 1995; Tinto, 1987, 1993).

It is also believed that these elite colleges and universities in some way facilitate participation in the highest social strata (Domhoff, 1983; Kingston and Lewis, 1990; Useem and Karabel, 1990; Zweigenhaft, 1993). In their study of three universities, one with students from highly educated and professional families, one with students from middle-class families, and one with a higher proportion of students' fathers holding manual labor positions, Hoffnung and

Sack (1981) found that at the highly selective institution, students were taught that social hierarchy is natural and unavoidable, and critical thinking, leadership, and intellectual growth were encouraged; at the less selective institutions with more middle-class and working-class students, students focused on vocational training. Moreover, the students at the highly selective institution were much more likely to plan on graduate degrees than at the two less selective institutions. They concluded that the highly selective institution prepared students for leadership, while the two less selective universities prepared students for followership. Youn et al. (1999), in their analysis of the social origins of American Rhodes scholars, found that Harvard, Yale, and Princeton produced one-third of these scholars. Attendance at one of those universities is correlated with upper-class family status according to their data.

Another reason these highly selective institutions are so successful is that they strengthen group identification and reinforce upper-class values, in part because upper-class students are often members of specific sororities, fraternities, and social clubs (Domhoff, 1983; Zweigenhaft, 1993). Accessing existing corporate and social networks and forming new ones through associations with other upper-class students is also thought to be a result of attending these institutions (Domhoff, 1983; Useem, 1994; Useem and Karabel, 1990; Zweigenhaft, 1993). The institutions do more than that, however: they also insulate their students from the outside world to a greater degree than many other colleges and universities do, and in many ways they are structured to prepare students to accept and shoulder the power and responsibility that is expected to accompany their higher educational and social status (Domhoff, 1983; Katchadourian and Boli, 1994).

These institutions are able to inculcate and reinforce upper-class values partly because they are attended disproportionately by high-SES and upper-class students (Astin, 1993; Hearn, 1984, 1990, 1991; Kingston and Lewis, 1990; Kingston and Smart, 1990; Martin et al., 2005). High-SES students gain access to elite institutions at higher rates than their low-SES peers due to high-quality academic preparation and by using several strategies when applying for admission (Astin, 1993; Bowen et al., 20005; Cookson and Persell, 1985; Domhoff, 1983; Hearn, 1984, 1990, 1991; Karabel, 2005; Kingston and Smart, 1990; Martin et al., 2005; McDonough, 1994, 1997; Persell and

Cookson, 1990; Persell, Catsambis, and Cookson, 1992; Zweigenhaft and Domhoff, 1991). Recently several scholars have written about this differential access (Bowen et al., 2005; Karabel, 2005). Low-income students currently comprise a tiny proportion of students at the nation's most selective institutions in part because the admissions systems at these institutions work to privilege high-income students in several ways.

The way in which merit is constructed privileges high-income students because it places weight on access to rigorous course work, grades, and test scores (Karabel, 2005). Early admission systems, legacy admits, admission based on athletic prowess (Karabel, 2005), and merit awards also work in concert to disadvantage low-income students in the admissions process (Heller and Rasmussen, 2002). High-SES students' admission strategies have changed over the past several decades; as college knowledge has become commodified, high-SES students have had access to the resources necessary to purchase test preparation, private college counseling, and other packaging advantages (McDonough et al., 2000). As a result of these practices, Bowen and colleagues (2005) call for a class-based affirmative action program to work in tandem with, not to replace, race-based affirmative action.

Since most EEC students do not attend these types of institutions, the educators at less selective institutions, which enroll the majority of low-income, first-generation, and low-SES students, must attempt to provide some of the attributes of highly selective colleges and universities that have the greatest effect on EEC students. The following sections provide an overview of the kinds of programs that have been found to assist EEC students in enrolling, persisting, and succeeding in college.

Programmatic Assistance

Several studies focused on making the issue of social class more visible on campus to students as a way to increase students' comfort levels on campus and their persistence. Borrego's dissertation (2001) examines three institutions' efforts at incorporating social class into their diversity discourses. She found that for the most part, issues of social class were explicitly included in the discourse around issues of access on all campuses and in the diversity discourse on two of the three campuses. One campus had parallel structures for incorporating conversations about race and ethnicity, on one hand, and social class, on the other, into the university's conversations and actions to reduce inequality, and the other two were working to incorporate social class directly into the diversity discourse. Initiatives at all three institutions were begun by individuals and subsequently received grant funding directed at supporting diversity and social class initiatives. Several people she interviewed believed that social class was often a hidden identity. Faculty were the most likely group on campuses to begin including social class in diversity discourses and partnerships with student affairs professionals could significantly improve students' experiences with and understanding of diversity.

Rodriguez (2003) believes that colleges and universities can help first-generation students succeed in several ways. Partnerships with local school districts can help provide all students with the information they need to make a successful transition from high school to college, including course requirements. Rodriguez also believes that college officials need to encourage students to be risk takers as they explore the unfamiliar terrain of a college campus.

Tett (2004) believes that elite institutions in particular need to examine the basic assumptions about the types of students they serve and the ways in which campuses are organized that alienate working-class students. Tett also believes that class structures and discourses need to shift to accommodate working-class students and that working-class students may benefit from classes that examine the social structure and provide them with language and other tools to critique that structure. Working-class students often face losses, due to family strains, when they pursue a college education, and educators need to recognize the risks these students face and help them manage their risks and balance their educational gains with their personal losses.

Ekman, Garth, and Noonan (2004) edited a collection of essays by college presidents whose institutions have successfully recruited, retained, and graduated low-income students. Although each story was unique, overall the institutions made an explicit, campuswide commitment to low-income or, in several cases, all students' success and followed that commitment with actions and decisions that supported students' success. Several started outreach efforts, often partnerships with local low-income school districts, to recruit students, and most were particularly careful to provide students with a range of holistic support services, especially in the first semester or year. The colleges and universities were flexible, scheduling classes that fit nontraditional students' schedules and offering alternative curricular structures, including online and accelerated course work.

Many of the programs described in Ekman, Garth and Noonan's work (2004) are similar to current government-sponsored and -funded college preparatory programs for underrepresented students. Many of these programs are held after school, on weekends, and during the summer. The federal government recognized the need for programmatic assistance for students and schools, instituting several programs beginning in the 1960s. Since then, programmatic solutions have been developed to address the challenges EEC students face in accessing an equitable opportunity to learn and subsequent college admission (Fenske, Geranios, Keller, and Moore, 1997; Gandara, 2002; Laguardia, 1998).

These programs, including Upward Bound, Gaining Early Awareness and Readiness for Undergraduate Programs (GEAR UP), and other state, local, and privately sponsored programs, typically begin working with students within the K-12 system to strengthen their academic experiences and assist them in making the transition to college (Burd, 2003; Blake, 1998; Fenske et al., 1997; Laguardia, 1998; McElroy and Armesto, 1998; Perna and Swail, 2001; Swail, 2000; Tierney and Jun, 2001; U.S. Department of Education, 2001). Studies of Upward Bound and other TRIO students have generally found that students in the programs have higher academic achievement than similar students who are not involved in such programs, but lower achievement levels than all students or more advantaged students (Balz and Esten, 1998; McLure and Child, 1998; U.S. Dept. of Education, 2003, 2004). Because of this, when these students enroll in college, they have an increased need for remedial or basic skills courses (Fenske et al., 1997). Bettinger and Long (2006) found that such remediation increased persistence and bachelor degree attainment.

Summer bridge programs are one solution universities have used to address the gap in preparation and achievement levels and to attract and retain underprepared students, most of whom are from low-SES or low income families or are the first in their families to attend college. Such programs typically provide academic preparation and transitional support in the summer prior to freshman year (Buck, 1985; Fitts, 1989; Logan, Salisbury-Glennon, and Spence, 2000; Perna, 2003; Perna and Swail, 2001; Swail and Perna, 2002; Valeri-Gold, Deming, and Stone, 1992). Studies have reported many positive effects of bridge program participation. Participating students achieve higher grades, stay in school longer, and have higher completion rates than comparable nonparticipants (Garcia, 1991; Evans, 1999; Obler, Francis, and Wishengrad, 2001; Pascarella and Terenzini, 2005). Furthermore, participants have increased locus of control, increased confidence, and increased self-esteem, important factors related to meeting the social and academic challenges of freshman year (Ackermann, 1991a; Fitts, 1989). Students who participate in bridge programs also have closer contact with other students and faculty during their freshman year and complete more core courses than nonprogram students (Ackermann, 1991a; Buck, 1985; Garcia, 1991; McLure and Child, 1998; Suhr, 1980). Moreover, students develop leadership ability, have more extensive involvement in the university community (Buck, 1985), and are more likely to turn to tutoring and counseling during the academic year than are their nonbridge peers (Fitts, 1989).

Because academic growth and achievement are a focus of bridge programs, these programs are often evaluated using students' GPA or achievement tests scores. Yet research has not consistently found significant differences between the GPA and achievement scores of EEC students attending bridge programs and similar students who do not attend (Ackermann, 1991b; Evans, 1999; Fitts, 1989; Logan et al., 2000; McLure and Child, 1998; Suhr, 1980). These inconsistencies may be due to the relatively short duration for most bridge programs, which may be insufficient to prepare some students for the rigors of college work.

Despite the lack of research evidence to support the efficacy of bridge programs on improving GPA and achievement scores, there is significant research support for the effects of bridge programs on retention (Ackermann, 1991a, 1991b; Balz and Esten, 1998; Buck, 1985; Garcia, 1991; Logan et al., 2000; McElroy and Armesto, 1998; Suhr, 1980; Valeri-Gold et al., 1992). Retention rates may be the most important factor regarding the efficacy of bridge programs. Students who benefit from bridge programs stay in college longer, take more credits, and graduate at higher rates than EEC students who do not attend bridge programs. Clearly these programs are highly effective at assisting EEC students with transitioning to, persisting at, and graduating from colleges and universities.

Conclusion

This chapter clearly illustrates the kinds of institutions, institutional features, and programming that promote EEC students' access to, progress through, and graduation from higher education institutions. These students need equitable admission practices, supportive environments, and academic skill assistance. The questions of how groups' interests are served are fundamental to increasing EEC students' college enrollment and graduation. Karabel (2005) writes that admission policies are designed to serve the interests of the privileged. However, maintaining a functioning opportunity structure is essential to the economic and social health of our country. As educators, we must work to reclaim and maintain such an opportunity structure.

Conclusions, Recommendations, and Implications for Practitioners, Policymakers, and Researchers

THE RESEARCH WE HAVE EXAMINED CLEARLY SHOWS THAT EEC students face obstacles in their preparation for, aspirations for, access to, persistence in, and graduation from college, as well as in their subsequent graduate school enrollment. Substantial research has found that these students face impediments, yet little has changed in recent decades despite a 30 percent gap between low- and high-income students' enrollment in college (Bedsworth et al., 2006) and attention from researchers and policymakers (Astin and Oseguera, 2004; Gladieux and Swail, 1998; McPherson and Schapiro, 1991). Disadvantages are documented as early as eighth grade (Adelman, 2006; Akerhielm et al., 1998) and accumulate throughout high school, into college, through college, and into graduate school and career paths. The literature is clear and compelling that these students have less access to rigorous course work in high school (Adelman, 2006; Akerhielm et al., 1998; Cabrera and La Nasa, 2000b, 2001; Martin et al., 2005; Oakes, 1985; Perna, 2000a; Terenzini et al., 2001), have less access to information about colleges and the process of applying (Cabrera and La Nasa, 2000b; Choy et al., 2000; Freeman, 1997, 1999; Horvat, 1996a, 1996b, 1997, 2003; Lynch and O'Riordan, 1998; McDonough, 1997; Terenzini et al., 2001; Walpole et al., 2005), apply less frequently (Martin et al., 2005; McDonough, 1997), attend less selective institutions (Astin and Oseguera, 2004; Cabrera et al., 2005; Hearn, 1984, 1990, 1991; Karabel and Astin, 1975; Karen, 1991; McDonough, 1997; Tinto, 2006; Titus, 2006a, 2006c), have less time to study and be involved in college because they are working more (Paulsen and St. John, 2002; Terenzini et al., 2001; Walpole, 2003), are less successful at persisting and graduating (Gladieux and Swail, 1998; Swail et al., 2004; Terenzini et al., 2001; Tinto, 2006; Titus, 2006a, 2006c), and attend graduate school less frequently (Goyette and Mullen, 2006; Terenzini et al., 2001, Walpole, 2003). The evidence documenting cumulative barriers in the college choice process, in persistence, and in attainment for EEC students is overwhelming; however, the evidence on differences in college experiences, particularly on knowledge gained in college and on aspirations, and on income discrepancies after college is currently insufficient to draw decisive conclusions. In addition to study results, the information I have presented provides a plethora of strategies and implications for researchers, policymakers, and practitioners.

Researchers

In order to more effectively address EEC students' needs, researchers should consistently include clear definitions of the students in the study sample, terms employed, and operationalization of variables, as well as consistently acknowledge the overlapping research areas focusing on these students. I suggested *economically and educationally challenged* (EEC) students as an umbrella term that encompasses low-SES, low-income, first-generation, and working-class students. Connecting these overlapping areas of research may lead to new insights. Such new insights are critical to increasing EEC students' representation in colleges and universities.

The multitude of definitions and terms used in research on EEC students, as well as the numerous ways variables are operationalized, are appropriate from a research perspective because most are relative definitions based on the study sample (Jencks et al., 1972, 1994). However, when researchers are investigating relative social standing, including information explaining the relative nature of SES measures and when the definitions of SES differ substantially from commonly accepted definitions, including explicit information regarding how and why they differ and how those differences affect the results and interpretation, could clarify and contextualize the sample and results. This information will assist novice researchers and, more important, practitioners who are working with EEC students in digesting and using the results.

More research is needed on EEC students' experiences in college, particularly on differential knowledge gains and aspirations, areas in which the research is scant. More work is also clearly needed on how experiences vary for students with multiple identities in ways that may affect their outcomes. Astin (1984, 1993) and Tinto (1987, 1993) have thoroughly documented the benefits of students' involvement and integration in college, and given the findings that EEC students are less involved in student organizations (Paulsen and St. John, 2002; Terenzini et al., 2001; Titus, 2006c; Walpole, 2003), further investigations of their levels of involvement and engagement are critical.

Studies focused on EEC student outcomes and the outcomes for students with multiple identities are also negligible and are critically necessary. Although Levine and Cureton (1998) bemoan the mitosis currently occurring on college campuses among racial, ethnic, gender, major, and sexual orientation groups, these differences among students have effects on their experiences and, hence, their outcomes. Pascarella and Terenzini (2005) believe investigating the differential effects of college for particular groups is one of the most urgent research needs in higher education.

Methodologically, the majority of the work is quantitative, drawing on national databases and regression. Given the complex nature of students' decisions, experiences, and outcomes, qualitative work may be particularly well suited to research on EEC students. Qualitative research focuses on context and meaning (Bogdan and Biklen, 2002) and may be uniquely suited to illuminating the ways in which structure and agency work in concert to produce distinct outcomes. Qualitative research could be particularly helpful in understanding students' decisions about cocurricular involvement because of the microlevel analysis that is possible.

Alternately, hierarchical linear modeling (HLM) shows promise because of its ability to tease apart nested data (Osborne, 2000), including the synergistic structural and agency variables. This methodological approach may be particularly helpful in taking multiple contexts into account, as recommended by Perna (2006). Perna and Titus (2004, 2005) have begun using HLM to examine the relative effects of student-level, school-level, and state-level variables. Regardless of the methodological approaches used, research designs have become more complex and measures more precise in an effort to account for students' experiences and decisions. Despite this increasing complexity, a substantial amount of variance is unaccounted for. Perhaps we need to consider new variables instead of trying to refine the variables we currently employ (Bowles and Gintis, 2002). Qualitative methods could provide a more emic approach to understanding students' experiences and decisions (Patton, 2002), and from that understanding new variables could be incorporated into study designs and frameworks.

In addition to incorporating new perspectives and variables, scholars working with specific conceptual frameworks could benefit from considering how their frameworks overlap with others. New theoretical insights could be gained from attempts at employing new frameworks to interpret results, perhaps through collaborations among scholars working with different frameworks. Such incorporations have occurred, with Perna (2000a, 2000b, 2004; 2006) and Perna and Titus (2004, 2005) incorporating cultural and social capital into human capital frameworks, with Paulsen and St. John's (2002) financial nexus model, and with recent work incorporating Bourdieu and critical race theory (McDonough et al., 2003; Walpole, 2004). Several structural variables are clearly important to incorporate into the more complex theoretical models, specifically financial aid variables, Bourdieuian cultural capital variables, and the racialized social structure with which students of color contend. Moreover, more attention to incorporating both these structural variables and students' agency will allow researchers to gain new insights. Such incorporation has begun and must be expanded to include a holistic set of influences. Caution must also be exercised, however, not to dilute the conceptual power of frameworks by employing them in piecemeal fashion. In addition to theoretical insights, examining the overlap in conceptual frameworks could result in new insights for policymakers.

Policymakers

Financial concerns play an enormous role in EEC students' decisions and experiences. Financial barriers exist at the federal, state, local, institutional, and individual levels, and all must be addressed in the effort to ease the burden on EEC students. On the federal level, the Spellings Commission concluded that financial barriers were significant for students and families seeking access to higher education (U.S. Department of Education, 2006). Research has consistently found that cost and access to financial aid shape students' access to and persistence in colleges and universities (Beattie, 2002; Cabrera et al., 1992; DesJardins et al., 2006; Fenske et al., 2000; Gladieux and Swail, 1998; Hwang, 2003; Paulsen and St. John, 1997, 2002; Perna and Titus, 2004; St. John et al., 2000; Terenzini et al., 2001). The Spellings report found that the financial aid process was confusing, unnecessarily lengthy, and poorly timed with students' decisions; others concur with this finding (Burd, 2006; Carnevale and Rose, 2004; U.S. Department of Education, 2006). In addition to process issues, the commission found that federal financial aid had not kept pace with college costs. An additional financial aid issue is that over the past several decades, financial aid has shifted from need-based to merit-based aid and from grants to loans, factors that hinder EEC students' participation (Carnevale and Rose, 2004; Dynarski, 2002; Heller and Rasmussen, 2002; Losing Ground, 2002; McPherson and Schapiro, 1991, 1998; Paulsen and St. John, 2002; St. John et al., 2000; Terenzini et al., 2001). These students have an increasing part of their need unmet by financial aid (Carnevale and Rose, 2004; McPherson and Schapiro, 1991, 1998; U.S. Department of Education, 2006), and they are further hindered by their reluctance to take out loans for their education (Burd, 2006; Carnevale and Rose, 2004). Overall, students are borrowing substantially more money to finance their education than they have in the past, which has negative implications for their future financial status (Losing Ground, 2002; U.S. Department of Education, 2006).

On the state level, state aid has typically decreased as a percentage of total budgets and has not kept pace with tuition increases (Burd, 2006; Carnevale and Rose, 2004; Losing Ground, 2002; Perna and Titus, 2004; U.S. Department of Education, 2006). Between 1992 and 2002, college attendance in all but two states became less affordable (Schmidt, 2004). The decreased state aid has put increased pressure on tuition, but the Spellings report also charges that institutions are not doing enough to control costs (U.S. Department of Education, 2006). Several scholars have made recommendations for increasing need-based aid and maintaining low tuition at public institutions (Carnevale and Rose, 2004; Paulsen and St. John, 2002; Perna and Titus, 2004; Terenzini et al., 2001). These recommendations include increasing the Pell grant to keep pace with inflation, streamlining and simplifying the financial aid application process, and instituting tuition cost-containment procedures. However given that many states are facing increasing budget pressures and given the country's current financial priorities, these recommendations seem unattainable.

Another policy issue in which some progress has been made is requiring a high school curriculum that will prepare students for the academic rigors of college (Kirst, Venezia, and Antonio, 2004; Measuring Up, 2006). Several scholars have noted the necessity of increasing the quality of the high school curriculum, particularly in math preparation (Adelman, 2006, Akerhielm et al., 1998; Cabrera and La Nasa, 2000b, 2001; Terenzini et al., 2001). According to the most recent data, students' high school preparation has improved, but substantial progress is still needed in this area. Although mandating a particular level of performance does not seem to have yet produced the desired results, finding other ways to increase students' academic achievement in high school and preparation for college is critical. Because the socioeconomic-based gaps in academic performance exist when students enter kindergarten, high-quality day care and preschool programs are needed. Programs such as these cannot be the only answer, however. Organizational reforms in schools, professional development for teachers, and raising the requirements for students all must work in concert to prepare students academically for college.

Practitioners

Although there are clear directions practitioners could take based on the study results reported in this volume, Kezar (2006) laments the fact that higher education research is not used sufficiently by practitioners to improve the educational process for students. Digesting and putting into practice much of the higher education research requires understanding the research process and some sophisticated methodological approaches. Although some practitioners have this understanding, many do not. Therefore, if educators want to improve educational access, experiences, and outcomes for EEC students, we must find outlets for translating our work into practitioner-friendly forms. Kezar suggests creating relationships with practitioner-focused professional organizations such as the National Association of Student Personnel Administrators. Undoubtedly partnerships with these organizations would be extremely helpful, but I think each of us should work to create links between our work and practitioners through publishing in practitioner journals, presenting at practitioner conferences, and engaging in discussion with practitioners on our own campuses. From the research outlined here, several interventions and strategies hold promise that can be implemented by many of us on our own campuses.

Students need access to rigorous course work in high school and to information about the college admissions process (Adelman, 2006; Akerhielm et al., 1998; McDonough, 1997; Terenzini et al., 2001; Walpole et al., 2005). In addition parental involvement is strongly supported in the research results as a key to high school academic achievement and college admission (Cabrera and La Nasa, 2000a, 2000c, 2001; Gandara, 1995; Hamrick and Stage, 2004; McCarron and Inkelas, 2006; Perna, 2000b; Terenzini et al., 2001). Practitioners can and should create partnerships with area schools to create clearer articulation between high school and college and provide information about choices, requirements, time lines, and financial aid. Some of these partnerships could evolve into the types of transition programs that have a demonstrated ability to attract and retain EEC students (Ackermann, 1991a, 1991b; Balz and Esten, 1998; Buck, 1985; Garcia, 1991; Logan et al., 2000; McElroy and Armesto, 1998; Suhr, 1980; Valeri-Gold et al., 1992). Practitioners should not have to work alone in forming these partnerships; faculty could also contribute expertise and talent. Both practitioners and faculty can also serve as mentors, which Levine and Nidiffer (1996) found important for students' college transitions.

Once students are admitted, institutions should work to ensure that students make a successful transition to the campus academically and socially. Involvement and integration are keys to this transition (Astin, 1984, 1993; Tinto, 1987, 1993), and practitioners can work with students to provide services and activities designed to engage them. Faculty and practitioners can encourage students to enroll in classes and majors in the traditional liberal arts disciplines, as well as encourage independent thinking, involvement, and leadership in cocurricular activities. This work belongs to all educators. Given everyone's busy schedules and lives, it is easier to believe that someone else is, or should be, assisting these students, but many students are not being helped into and through our institutions in ways that promote their persistence, graduation, and graduate school enrollment.

Economically and educationally challenged students face significant structural impediments and often make decisions that differ from educators' recommendations and from their peers' decisions, yet there are many low-SES, low-income, first-generation, and working-class students who do manage to surmount the barriers and make decisions that result in persistence and attainment. As educators, we must learn from the successful students in order to minimize the obstacles and advocate for and assist students with their decisions all along the educational pipeline.

References

Abbott, J. (1965). Students' social class in three northern universities. *British Journal of Sociology, 16*(3), 206–220.

Ackermann, S. P. (1991a). The benefits of summer bridge programs for underrepresented and low-income students. *College and University, 66*(4), 201–208.

Ackermann, S. P. (1991b). The benefits of summer bridge programs for underrepresented and low-income transfer students. *Community/Junior College, 15*, 211–224.

Adelman, C. (2006). *The toolbox revisited.* Washington, DC: U.S. Department of Education.

Akerhielm, K., Berger, J., Hooker, M., and Wise, D. (1998). *Factors related to college enrollment: Final report.* Washington, DC: U.S. Department of Education.

Allen, W. R., and Haniff, N. Z. (1991). Race, gender and academic performance in U.S. higher education. In W. R Allen, E. G. Epps, and N. Z. Haniff (Eds.), *College in black and white: African American students in predominantly white and in historically black public universities.* Albany: State University of New York Press.

Allmendinger, D. (1975). *Paupers and scholars: The transformation of student life in 19th century New England.* New York: St. Martin's Press.

Anderson, M. S., and Hearn, J. C. (1992). Equity issues in higher education outcomes. In W. E. Becker and D. R. Lewis (Eds.), *The economics of American higher education* (pp. 301–334). Norwell, MA: Kluwer.

Archer, L., and Hutchings, M. (2000). "Bettering yourself"? Discourses of risk, cost, and benefit in ethnically diverse, young working class non-participants' constructions of higher education. *British Journal of Sociology of Education, 21*(4), 555–574.

Arzy, M. R., Davies, T. G., and Harbour, C. P. (2006). Low income students: Their lived university campus experiences pursuing baccalaureate degrees with private foundation scholarship assistance. *College Student Journal, 40*(4), 750–766.

Astin, A. W. (1975). *Preventing students from dropping out.* San Francisco: Jossey-Bass.

Astin, A. W. (1984). Student involvement: A developmental theory for higher education. *Journal of College Student Personnel, 25*(4), 297–307.

Astin, A. W. (1985). Expanding the quantity and quality of educational opportunities. In A. W. Astin (Ed.), *Achieving educational excellence.* San Francisco: Jossey-Bass.

Astin, A. W. (1993). *What matters in college? Four critical years revisited.* San Francisco: Jossey-Bass.

Astin, A. W. (1999). How the liberal arts college affects students. *Daedalus, 128*(1), 77–100.

Astin, A. W., and Oseguera, L. (2004). The declining "equity" of American higher education. *Review of Higher Education, 27*(3), 321–341.

Ball, S. J., Reay, D., and David, M. (2002). "Ethnic choosing": Minority ethnic students, social class, and higher education choice. *Race, Ethnicity, and Education, 5*(4), 333–357.

Balz, F. J., and Esten, M. R. (1998). Fulfilling private dreams, serving public priorities: An analysis of TRIO students' success at independent colleges and universities. *Journal of Negro Education, 67*(4), 333–345.

Beattie, I. R. (2002). Are all "adolescent econometricians" created equal? Racial, class, and gender differences in college enrollment. *Sociology of Education, 75,* 19–43.

Becker, G. S. (1993). *Human capital: A theoretical and empirical analysis with special reference to education* (3rd ed.). Chicago: University of Chicago Press.

Bedsworth, W., Colby, S., and Doctor, J. (2006). *Reclaiming the American dream.* Retrieved March 12, 2007, from http://www.bridgespangroup.org/kno_articles_americandream.html.

Berger, J. B., Milem, J. F., and Paulsen, M. B. (1998). *The exploration of "habitus" as a multi-dimensional construct.* Paper presented at the annual meeting of the Association for the Study of Higher Education. Miami.

Bettinger, E. P., and Long, B. T. (2006). *Addressing the needs of under-prepared students in higher education: Does college remediation work?* Retrieved March 16, 2007, from http://gseacademic.harvard.edu/~longbr.

Blake, J. H. (1998). The full circle: TRIO programs, higher education and the American future: Toward a new vision of democracy. *Journal of Negro Education, 67*(4), 329–332.

Blau, P. M. (1992). Mobility and status attainment. *Contemporary Sociology, 21*(5), 596–598.

Blau, P. M., and Duncan, O. D. (1967). *The occupational structure.* Hoboken, NJ: Wiley.

Blau, P. M., Duncan, O. D., and Tyree, A. (1994). The process of stratification. In D. B. Grusky (Ed.), *Social stratification: Class, race, and gender in sociological perspective* (pp. 390–402). Boulder, CO.: Westview Press.

Boatsman, K. C. (1995). *Predicting American college student degree aspirations: The role of cultural, social and economic capital.* Unpublished manuscript, University of California, Los Angeles.

Bogdan, R., and Biklen, S. (2002). *Qualitative research for education* (2nd ed.). Needham Heights, MA: Allyn & Bacon.

Bohon, S. A., Johnson, M. K., and Gorman, B. K. (2006). College aspirations and expectations among Latino adolescents in the United States. *Social Problems, 53*(2), 207–225.

Borrego, S. E. (2001). *Expanding the diversity conversation: The emergence of working class culture.* Unpublished doctoral dissertation, Claremont Graduate University.

Bourdieu, P. (1977). Cultural reproduction and social reproduction. In J. Karabel and A. H. Halsey (Eds.), *Power and ideology in education* (pp. 487–511). New York: Oxford University Press.

Bourdieu, P. (1990). Artistic taste and cultural capital. In J. Alexander and S. Seidman, (Eds.), *Culture and society: Contemporary debates* (pp. 205–215). Cambridge: Cambridge University Press.

Bourdieu, P. (1994). Distinction: A social critique. In D. B. Grusky (Ed.), *Social stratification: Class, race, and gender in sociological perspective* (pp. 499–525). Boulder, CO: Westview Press.

Bowen, W. G., and Bok, D. (1998). *The shape of the river: Long-term consequences of considering race in college and university admissions.* Princeton, NJ: Princeton University Press.

Bowen, W. G., Kurzweil, M., and Tobin, E. (2005). *Equity and excellence in American higher education.* Charlottesville: University of Virginia Press.

Bowles, S., and Gintis, H. (1976). *Schooling in capitalist America.* New York: Basic Books.

Bowles, S., and Gintis, H. (2002). The inheritance of inequality. *Journal of Economic Perspectives, 16*(3), 3–30.

Brint, S., and Karabel, J. (1989). *The diverted dream: Community colleges and the promise of educational opportunity in America, 1900–1985.* New York: Oxford University Press.

Buck, J. (1985, February). *Summer bridge: A residential learning experience for high risk freshmen at the University of California, San Diego.* Paper presented at the Fourth Annual Conference on the Freshman Year Experience, University of Columbia, SC.

Burd, S. (2003, March 14). Programs for disadvantaged students feud over their futures. *Chronicle of Higher Education, 49*(27), A21–A22.

Burd, S. (2006, June 9). Working class students feel the pinch. *Chronicle of Higher Education,* A20–A24.

Cabrera, A. F., Burkum, K. R., and La Nasa, S. M. (2005). Pathways to a four-year degree: Determinants of transfer and degree completion. In A. Seidman (Ed.), *College student retention: A formula for student success.* Westport, CT: ACE/Praeger.

Cabrera, A. F., and La Nasa, S. M. (2000a). Understanding the college choice process. In A. F. Cabrera and S. M. La Nasa (Eds.), *Understanding the college choice process of disadvantaged students* (pp. 5–22). San Francisco: Jossey-Bass.

Cabrera, A. F., and La Nasa, S. M. (2000b). Three critical tasks America's disadvantaged face on their path to college. In A. F. Cabrera and S. M. La Nasa (Eds.), *Understanding the college choice process of disadvantaged students* (pp. 23–29). San Francisco: Jossey-Bass.

Cabrera, A. F., and La Nasa, S. M. (2000c). Overcoming the tasks on the path to college for America's disadvantaged. In A. F. Cabrera and S. M. La Nasa (Eds.), *Understanding the college choice process of disadvantaged students* (pp. 31–43). San Francisco: Jossey-Bass.

Cabrera, A. F., and La Nasa, S. M. (2001). On the path to college: Three critical tasks facing America's disadvantaged. *Research in Higher Education, 42*(2), 119–149.

Cabrera, A. F., Nora, A., and Castaneda, M. B. (1992). The role of finances in the persistence process: A structural model. *Research in Higher Education, 33*(5), 571–593.

Cabrito, B. G. (2004). Higher education: An education for the elites? The Portuguese case. *Higher Education in Europe, 29*(1), 33–45.

Carnevale, A. P., and Rose, S. J. (2004). Socioeconomic status, race/ethnicity, and selective college admissions. In R. D. Kahlenberg (Ed.), *America's untapped resource: Low-income students in higher education* (pp. 101–156). New York: Century Foundation Press.

Carter, D. J. (1999) The impact of institutional choice and environments on African American and white students' degree expectations. *Research in Higher Education, 40*(1), 17–41.

Carter, P. L. (2003). "Black" cultural capital, status positioning, and schooling conflicts for low-income African American youth. *Social Problems, 50*(1), 136–155.

Casey, J. G. (2005). Diversity, discourse, and the working-class student. *Academe, 91*(4), 33–36.

Choy, S. P., Horn, L. J., Nunez, A., and Chen, X. (2000). Transition to college: What helps at-risk students and students whose parents did not attend colleges. *New Directions for Institutional Research, 2000*(107), 45–63.

Cicourel, A. V., and Kitsuse, J. I. (1963). *The educational decision makers.* Indianapolis: Bobbs-Merrill.

Clark, B. (1960). The "cooling out" function in higher education. *American Journal of Sociology, 65,* 569–576.

Coleman, J. S. (1988). Social capital in the creation of human capital. *American Journal of Sociology, 94,* S95–S120.

Conley, D. (1999–2000). Getting into the black: Race, wealth, and public policy. *Political Science Quarterly, 114*(4), 595–612.

Conley, D. (2001). Capital for college: Parental assets and postsecondary schooling. *Sociology of Education, 74*(1), 59–72.

Connor, H. (2001). Deciding for or against participation in higher education: The views of young people from lower social class backgrounds. *Higher Education Quarterly, 55*(2), 204–224.

Cookson Jr., P. W., and Persell, C. (1985). *Preparing for power: America's elite boarding schools.* New York: Basic Books.

Corcoran, M. 1995. Rags to rags: Poverty and mobility in the United States. *Annual Review of Sociology, 21,* 237–267.

Dale, S. B., and Krueger, A. B. (2002). Estimating the payoff of attending a more selective college: An application of selection on observables and unobservables. *Quarterly Journal of Economics, 107*(4), 1491–1527.

Davies, S., and Guppy, N. (1997). Fields of study, college selectivity, and student inequalities in higher education. *Social Forces, 75,* 1417–1438.

Davis, J. E. (1998). Cultural capital and the role of historically black colleges and universities in educational reproduction. In K. Freeman (Ed.), *African American culture and heritage in higher education research and practice.* Westport, CT: Praeger.

Dennis, J. M., Phinney, J. S., and Chuateco, L. I. (2005). The role of motivation, parental support, and peer support in the academic success of ethnic minority first generation college students. *Journal of College Student Development, 46*(3), 223–236.

DesJardins, S. L., Ahlburg, D. A., and McCall, B. P. (2006). An integrated model of application, admission, enrollment, and financial aid. *Journal of Higher Education, 77*(3), 381–429.

Dixson, A. D., and Rousseau, C. K. (2005). And we are still not saved: Critical race theory in education ten years later. *Race, Ethnicity and Education, 8*(1), 7–27.

Domhoff, G. W. (1983). *Who rules America now?* New York: Simon and Schuster.

Dynarski, S. (2002). Race, income, and the impact of merit aid. In D. E. Heller and P. Marin (Eds.), *Who should we help? The negative social consequences of merit scholarships.* Cambridge, MA: Civil Rights Project, Harvard University.

Egerton, M. (2001). Mature graduates II: Occupational attainment and the effects of social class. *Oxford Review of Education, 27*(2), 271–286.

Egerton, M., and Halsey, A. H. (1993). Trends by social class and gender in access to higher education in Britain. *Oxford Review of Education, 19*(2), 183–197.

Ekman, R., Garth, R., and Noonan, J. F. (2004). Introduction. In R. Ekman, R. Garth, and J. F. Noonan (Eds.), *Powerful partnerships: Independent colleges share high-impact strategies for low income students' success* (pp. 1–6). Lumina Foundation New Agenda Series, 5(4). Indianapolis, IN: Lumina Foundation. Retrieved August 27, 2007, from http://www.luminafoundation.org/publications/newagenda.html.

Evans, R. (1999). A comparison of success indicators for program and nonprogram participants in a community college summer bridge program for minority students. *Visions, 2*(2), 6–14.

Farmer, H. (1978). Career counseling implications for the lower social class and women. *Personnel and Guidance Journal, 56*(8), 467–471.

Fenske, R. H., Geranios, C. A., Keller, J. E., and Moore, D. E. (1997). Early intervention programs: Opening the door to higher education. (ASHE-ERIC Higher Education Report, Vol. 25, No. 6). Washington, DC: ERIC Clearinghouse on Higher Education. (ED 412 863).

Fenske, R. H., Porter, J. D., DuBrock, C. P. (2000). Tracking financial aid and persistence of women, minority, and needy students in science, engineering, and mathematics. *Research in Higher Education, 41*(1), 67–94.

Filkins, J. W., and Doyle, S. K. (2002). *First generation and low income students: Using the NSSE data to study effective educational practices and students' self-reported gains.* Paper presented at the annual meeting of the Association for Institutional Research, Toronto, Canada.

Fitts, J.D. (1989). *A comparison of locus of control and achievement among remedial summer bridge and nonbridge students in community colleges in New Jersey.* Trenton, NJ: New Jersey Department of Higher Education. (ERIC Document Reproduction Service No. ED315102).

Fleming, J. (1984). *Blacks in college.* San Francisco: Jossey-Bass.

Freeland, R. M. (1997). A world transformed: A golden age for American universities, 1945–1970. In L. F. Goodchild and H. S. Wechsler (Eds.), *The history of higher education* (2nd ed., pp. 587–609). Boston: Pearson Custom Publishing.

Freeman, K. (1997). Increasing African Americans' participation in higher education: African American high-school students' perspectives. *Journal of Higher Education, 68,* 523–550.

Freeman, K. (1999). The race factor in African Americans' college choice. *Urban Education, 34*(1), 4–25.

Gandara, P. (1995). *Over the ivy walls: The educational mobility of low-income Chicanos.* Albany: State University of New York Press.

Gandara, P. (2002). Meeting common goals: Linking K-12 and college interventions. In W. G. Tierney and L. S. Hagedorn (Eds.), *Increasing access to college* (pp. 81–103). Albany: State University of New York Press.

Garcia, P. (1991). Summer bridge: Improving retention rates for underprepared students. *Journal of the First-Year Experience and Students in Transition, 3*(2), 91–105.

Gaskell, J. (1985). Course enrollment in the high school: The perspective of working-class females. *Sociology of Education. 58,* 48–59.

Gibbons, M. M., and Shoffner, M. F. (2004). Prospective first-generation college students: Meeting their needs through social cognitive career theory. *Professional School Counseling, 8*(1), 91–98.

Gilbert, D., and Kahl, J. (1993). *The American class structure* (4th ed.). New York: Wadsworth.

Gladieux, L. E., and Swail, W. S. (1998). *Financial aid is not enough: Improving the odds of college success.* Princeton, NJ: College Board.

Goldrick-Rab, S., and Han, S. W. (2006). *The "class gap" in the "gap year": High school course-taking and the transition to college.* Paper presented at the annual meeting of the American Educational Research Association, San Francisco.

Goldstein, M. S. (1974). Academic careers and vocational choices of elite and non-elite students at elite colleges. *Sociology of Education, 47*(4), 491–510.

Goyette, K. A., and Mullen, A. L. (2006). Who studies the arts and sciences? Social background and the choice and consequences of undergraduate field of study. *Journal of Higher Education, 77*(3), 497–538.

Hacker, A. (1995). *Two nations: Black and white, separate, hostile, unequal.* New York: Ballantine Books.

Hagedorn, L. S., Lester, J., Moon, H. S., and Tibbetts, K. (2006). Native Hawaiian community college students: What happens? *Community College Journal of Research and Practice, 30*(1), 21–39.

Halle, D. (1984). *America's working man.* Chicago: University of Chicago Press.

Hamrick, F. A., and Stage, F. K. (2004). College predisposition at high minority enrollment, low income schools. *Review of Higher Education, 27*(2), 151–168.

Harker, R. K. (1984). On reproduction, habitus, and education. *British Journal of Sociology of Education, 5,* 117–127.

Hearn, J. C. (1984). The relative roles of academic, ascribed, and socioeconomic characteristics in college destinations. *Sociology of Education, 57*(1), 22–30.

Hearn, J. C. (1990). Pathways to attendance at the elite colleges. In P. W. Kingston and L. S. Lewis (Eds.), *The high-status track: Studies of elite schools and stratification.* Albany: State University of New York Press.

Hearn, J. C. (1991). Academic and nonacademic influences on the college destinations of 1980 high school graduates. *Sociology of Education, 64,* 158–171.

Heller, D. E., and Rasmussen, C. J. (2002). Merit scholarships and college access: Evidence from Florida and Michigan. In D. E. Heller and P. Marin (Eds.), *Who should we help? The negative social consequences of merit scholarships.* Cambridge, MA: Civil Rights Project at Harvard University.

Hoffnung, R. J., and Sack, A. L. (1981). *Does higher education reduce or reproduce social class differences? Schooling at Yale University, University of Connecticut, and University of New Haven, and student attitudes and expectations regarding future work.* Paper presented at the annual meeting of the Eastern Psychological Association, New York.

Horn, L. (2006). *Placing graduation rates in context: How 4-year college graduation rates vary with selectivity and the size of low-income enrollment* (NCES 2007–161). Washington, DC: National Center for Education Statistics.

Horvat, E. M. (1996a). *African American students and college choice decisionmaking in social context: The influence of race and class on educational opportunity.* Paper presented at the annual meeting of the American Educational Research Association, New York.

Horvat, E. M. (1996b). *Boundaries of belonging and postsecondary access: African American students and college choice decisionmaking in social context.* Paper presented at the annual meeting of the Association for the Study of Higher Education, Memphis, TN.

Horvat, E. M. (1997). *Structure, standpoint, and practices: The construction and meaning of the boundaries of blackness for African American female high school seniors in the college choice process.* Paper presented at the annual meeting of the American Educational Research Association, Chicago.

Horvat, E. M. (2001). Understanding equity and access in higher education: The potential contribution of Pierre Bourdieu. In J. Smart (Ed.), *Higher education: Handbook of theory and research, Vol. 16.* Edison, NJ: Agathon Press.

Horvat, E. M. (2003). The interactive effects of race and class in educational research: Theoretical insights from the work of Pierre Bourdieu. *Penn GSE Perspectives on Urban Education, 2*(1). Retrieved August 27, 2007, from http://www.urbanedjournal.org/archive/index.html.

Horvat, E. M., and Antonio, A. L. (1999). "Hey, those shoes are out of uniform": African American girls in an elite high school and the importance of habitus. *Anthropology and Education Quarterly, 30*(3), 317–342.

Hossler, D., and Maple, S. (1993). Being undecided about postsecondary education. *Review of Higher Education, 16*(3), 285–307.

Hossler, D., Schmit, J., and Vesper, N. (1999). *Going to college: How social, economic, and educational factors influence the decisions students make.* Baltimore, MD: Johns Hopkins University Press.

Hurtado, S., Inkelas, K. K., Briggs, C., and Rhee, B. (1997). Differences in college access and choice among racial/ethnic groups: Identifying continuing barriers. *Research in Higher Education, 38*(1), 43–75.

Hwang, D. (2003). *The impact of financial aid on persistence: Application of the financial nexus model.* Unpublished doctoral dissertation, University of North Texas.

Ishitani, T. T. (2006). Studying attrition and degree completion behavior among first generation college students in the United States. *Journal of Higher Education, 77*(5), 861–884.

Jackman, M. R. and Jackman, R. W. (1983). *Class awareness in the United States.* Berkeley: University of California Press.

Jackson, L. R. (1998). The influence of both race and gender on the experiences of African American college women. *The Review of Higher Education, 21*(4), 359–375.

Jencks, C., Bartlett, S., Corcoran, M., Crouse, J., Eaglesfield, D., Jackson, G., et al. (1979). *Who gets ahead? The determinants of economic success in America.* New York: Basic Books.

Jencks, C., Smith, M., Acland, H., Bane, M. J., Cohen, D., Gintis, H., et al. (1972). *Inequality: A reassessment of the effect of family and schooling in America.* New York: Basic Books.

Jencks, C., Smith, M., Acland, H., Bane, M. J., Cohen, D., Gintis, H., et al. (1994). Inequality: A reassessment of the effect of family and schooling in America. In D. B. Grusky (Ed.), *Social stratification: Class, race, and gender in sociological perspective* (pp. 403–409). Boulder, CO: Westview Press.

Karabel, J. (1972). Community colleges and social stratification. *Harvard Educational Review, 42,* 521–562.

Karabel, J. (2005). *The chosen: The hidden history of admission and exclusion at Harvard, Yale, and Princeton.* Boston: Houghton Mifflin.

Karabel, J., and Astin, A. W. (1975). Social class, academic ability, and college quality. *Social Forces, 53*(3), 381–398.

Karen, D. (1991). The politics of class, race, and gender: Access to higher education in the United States, 1960–1986. *American Journal of Education, 99,* 208–237.

Katchadourian, H., and Boli, J. (1994). *Cream of the crop: The impact of elite education in the decade after college.* New York: Basic Books.

Kezar, A. (2006). Perspective: Even if the trees have no fruit, no one will ever know. *ASHE Newsletter, 19*(3), 3–4.

Kiang, P. N. (1992). Issues of curriculum and community for first generation Asian Americans in college. In L. S. Zwerling and H. B. London (Eds.), *First generation students: Confronting the cultural issues* (pp. 97–112). San Francisco: Jossey-Bass.

Kingston, P. W., and Lewis, L. S. (1990). Undergraduates at elite institutions: The best, the brightest, and the richest. In P. W. Kingston and L. S. Lewis (Eds.), *The high status track: Studies of elite schools and stratification.* Albany: State University of New York Press.

Kingston, P. W., and Smart, J. C. (1990). The economic pay-off of prestigious colleges. In P. W. Kingston and L. S. Lewis (Eds.), *The high status track: Studies of elite schools and stratification.* Albany: State University of New York Press.

Kirst, M. W., Venezia, A., and Antonio, A. L. (2004). What have we learned, and where do we go next? In M. W. Kirst and A. Venezia (Eds.), *From high school to college: Improving opportunities for success in postsecondary education* (pp. 285–319). San Francisco: Jossey-Bass.

Kohn, M. (1977). *Class and conformity.* Chicago: University of Chicago Press.

Ladson-Billings, G. (2005). The evolving role of critical race theory in educational scholarship. *Race, Ethnicity and Education, 8*(1), 115–119.

Ladson-Billings, G., and Tate IV, W. F. (1995). Toward a critical race theory of education. *Teachers College Record, 97*(1), 47–68.

Laguardia, A. (1998). A survey of school/college partnerships for minority and disadvantaged students. *Urban Review, 30*(2), 167–186.

Lamont, M., and Lareau, A. (1988). Cultural capital: Allusions, gaps, and glissandos in recent theoretical developments. *Sociological Theory, 6,* 153–168.

Lara, J. (1992). Reflections: Bridging cultures. In L. S. Zwerling and H. B. London (Eds.), *First generation students: Confronting the cultural issues* (pp. 65–70). San Francisco: Jossey-Bass.

Lareau, A. (1987). Social class differences in family-school relationships: The importance of cultural capital. *Sociology of Education, 60,* 73–85.

Lareau, A. (1993). *Home advantage: Social class and parental intervention in elementary education.* Philadelphia: Falmer Press.

Lareau, A., and Weininger, E. B. (2003). Cultural capital in educational research: A critical assessment. *Theory and Society, 32,* 567–606.

Levine, A., and Cureton, J. S. (1998). *When hope and fear collide: A portrait of today's college students.* San Francisco: Jossey-Bass.

Levine, A., and Nidiffer, J. (1996). *Beating the odds: How the poor get to college.* San Francisco: Jossey-Bass.

Littrell, B. (1999). The liberal arts and the working classes. *Peace Review, 11*(2), 267–273.

Logan, C. R., Salisbury-Glennon, J., and Spence, L. D. (2000). The Learning Edge Academic Program: Toward a community of learners. *Journal of the First-Year Experience and Students in Transition, 12*(1), 77–104.

London, H. B. (1992). Transformations: Cultural challenges faced by first generation students. In L. S. Zwerling and H. B. London (Eds.), *First generation students: Confronting the cultural issues* (pp. 5–11). San Francisco: Jossey-Bass.

Long, B. T. (2007). The contributions of economists to the study of college access and success. *Teachers College Record, 109*(10). Retrieved March 16, 2007, from http://gseacademic.harvard.edu/~longbr.

Losing ground: A national status report on the affordability of American higher education. (2002). San Jose, CA: National Center for Public Policy and Higher Education.

Luzzo, D. A. (1992). Ethnic group and social class differences in college students' career development. *Career Development Quarterly, 41*(2), 161–173.

Lynch, K., and O'Riordan, C. (1998). Inequality in higher education: A study of class barriers. *British Journal of Sociology of Education, 19*(4), 445–478.

MacLeod, J. (1987). *Ain't no makin' it: The leveled aspirations of a low-income neighborhood.* Boulder, CO: Westview Press.

Manski, C. F., and Wise, D. A. (1983). *College choice in America.* Cambridge, MA: Harvard University Press.

Marks, A., Turner, E., and Osborne, M. (2003). "Not for the likes of me": The overlapping effect of social class and gender factors in the decision made by adults not to participate in higher education. *Journal of Further and Higher Education, 27*(4), 347–364.

Martin, I., Karabel, J., and Jaquez, S. W. (2005). High school segregation and access to the University of California. *Educational Policy, 19*(2), 308–330.

Marx, K. (1956). Social classes and class conflict. In T. B. Bottomore and M. Rubel (Eds.), *Karl Marx: Selected writings in sociology and social philosophy.* New York: McGraw-Hill.

McCarron, G. P., and Inkelas, K. K. (2006). The gap between educational aspirations and attainment for first-generation college students and the role of parental involvement. *Journal of College Student Development, 47*(5), 534–549.

McDonough, P. M. (1994). Buying and selling higher education. *Journal of Higher Education, 65,* 427–446.

McDonough, P. M. (1997). *Choosing colleges: How social class and schools structure opportunity.* Albany: State University of New York Press.

McDonough, P. M., and Antonio, A. L. (1996). *Ethnic and racial differences in selectivity of college choice.* Paper presented at the annual meeting of the American Educational Research Association, New York.

McDonough, P. M., Antonio, A. L., and Trent, J. (1997). Black students, black colleges: An African American college-choice model. *Journal for a Just and Caring Education, 3,* 9–36.

McDonough, P. M., Nunez, A., Ceja, M., and Solarzano, D. (2003). *A model of Latino college choice.* Paper presented at the annual meeting of the Association for the Study of Higher Education, Portland, OR.

McDonough, P. M., Ventresca, M., and Outcault, C. (2000). Field of dreams: Organizational field approaches to understanding the transformation of college access, 1965–1995. In J. Smart (Ed.), *Higher education: Handbook of theory and research, Vol. 15.* Edison, NJ: Agathon Press.

McElroy, E. J., and Armesto, M. (1998). TRIO and Upward Bound: History, programs, and issues: Past, present, and future. *Journal of Negro Education, 67*(4), 373–381.

McLure, G. T., and Child, R. L. (1998). Upward bound students compared to other college-bound students: Profiles of nonacademic characteristics and academic achievement. *Journal of Negro Education, 67*(4), 346–363.

McNamee, S. J., and Miller Jr., R. K. (2004). *The meritocracy myth.* Lanham, MD: Rowman and Littlefield.

McPherson, M. S., and Schapiro, M. O. (1991). *Keeping college affordable: Government and educational opportunity.* Washington, DC: Brookings Institute.

McPherson, M. S., and Schapiro, M. O. (1998). *The student aid game: Meeting need and rewarding talent in American higher education.* Princeton, NJ: Princeton University Press.

Measuring up: The national report card on higher education. (2006). San Jose, CA: National Center for Public Policy and Higher Education.

Montelongo, R. (2003). *Latino/a undergraduate involvement with college student organizations and its effects on specific student outcomes at two large, predominately white, midwestern universities.* Paper presented at the annual meeting of the American Educational Research Association, Chicago.

Nettles, M. T., and Perna, L. W. (1997). *The African American education data book, Volume 1. Higher and adult education.* Fairfax, VA: Frederick D. Patterson Research Institute.

Nunez, A., and Cuccaro-Alamin, S. (1998). *First-generation students: Undergraduates whose parents never enrolled in postsecondary education.* Washington, DC: U.S. Department of Education.

Nunez, A., McDonough, P. M., Ceja, M., and Solorzano, D. (2004). *Ethnicities and Latina/o college choice.* Paper presented at the annual meeting of Association for the Study of Higher Education, Kansas City, MO.

Oakes, J. (1985). *Keeping track: How schools structure inequality.* New Haven, CT: Yale University Press.

Obler, M., Francis, K., and Wishengrad, R. (2001). Combining of traditional counseling, instruction, and mentoring functions with academically deficient college freshmen. *Journal of Educational Research, 70*(3), 142–147.

O'Dair, S. (2003). Class work: Site of egalitarian activism or site of embourgeoisement? *College English, 65*(6), 593–607.

Osborne, J. W. (2000). Advantages of hierarchical linear modeling. *Practical Assessment, Research and Evaluation, 7*(1). Retrieved March 19, 2007, from http://PAREonline.net /getvn.asp?v=7andn=1.

Pascarella, E. T., Pierson, C. T., Wolniak, G. C., and Terenzini, P. T. (2004). First-generation college students: Additional evidence on college experiences and outcomes. *Journal of Higher Education, 75*(3), 249–284.

Pascarella, E. T., and Terenzini, P. T. (1991). *How college affects students.* San Francisco: Jossey-Bass.

Pascarella E. T., and Terenzini, P. T. (2005). *How college affects students, Vol. 2. A third decade of research.* San Francisco: Jossey-Bass.

Patton, M. Q. (2002). *Qualitative research and evaluation methods* (3rd ed.). Thousand Oaks, CA: Sage.

Paulsen, M. B., and St. John, E. P. (1997). The financial nexus between college choice and persistence. In R. A. Voorhees (Ed.), *Researching student aid: Creating an action agenda* (pp. 65–82). San Francisco: Jossey-Bass.

Paulsen, M. B., and St. John, E. P. (2002). Social class and college costs: Examining the financial nexus between college choice and persistence. *Journal of Higher Education, 73*(2), 189–236.

Perna, L. W. (2000a). Differences in the decision to attend college among African Americans, Hispanics, and whites. *Journal of Higher Education, 71*(2), 117–141.

Perna, L. W. (2000b). Racial and ethnic group differences in college enrollment decisions. In A. F. Cabrera and S. M. La Nasa (Eds.), *Understanding the college choice process of disadvantaged students* (pp. 65–83). San Francisco: Jossey- Bass.

Perna, L. W. (2003). *The key to college access: A rigorous college preparatory curriculum.* Paper presented at the annual meeting of the American Educational Research Association, Chicago.

Perna, L. W. (2004). Understanding the decision to enroll in graduate school: Sex and racial/ethnic group differences. *Journal of Higher Education, 75*(5), 487–527.

Perna, L. W. (2005). The benefits of higher education: Sex, racial/ethnic, and socioeconomic group differences. *Review of Higher Education, 29*(1), 23–52.

Perna, L. W. (2006). Studying college access and choice: A proposed conceptual model. In J. C. Smart (Ed.), *Higher education: Handbook of theory and research* (Vol. 21, pp. 99–157). New York: Springer,

Perna, L. W., and Swail, W. S. (2001). Pre-college outreach and early intervention programs: An approach to achieving equal educational opportunity. *Thought and Action, 17*(1), 99–110.

Perna, L. W., and Titus, M. A. (2004). Understanding differences in the choice of college attended: The role of state public policies. *Review of Higher Education, 27*(4), 501–525.

Perna, L. W., and Titus, M. A. (2005). The relationship between parental involvement as social capital and college enrollment: An examination of racial/ethnic group differences. *Journal of Higher Education, 76*(5), 485–518.

Persell, C., Catsambis, S., and Cookson, P. (1992). Differential asset conversion: Class and gendered pathways to selective colleges. *Sociology of Education, 65,* 208–225.

Persell, C., and Cookson Jr., P. (1990). Chartering and bartering: Elite education and social reproduction. In P. W. Kingston and L. S. Lewis (Eds.), *The high status track: Studies of elite schools and stratification.* Albany: State University of New York Press.

Pike, G. R., and Kuh, G. D. (2005). First- and second-generation college students: A comparison of their engagement and intellectual development. *Journal of Higher Education, 76*(3), 276–300.

Rendon, L. I. (1992). From the barrio to the academy: Revelations of a Mexican American "scholarship girl." In L. S. Zwerling and H. B. London (Eds.), *First generation students: Confronting the cultural issues* (pp. 55–64). San Francisco: Jossey-Bass.

Rodriguez, S. (2003, September–October). What helps some first generation students succeed? *About Campus,* 17–22.

Rouse, C. E. (1994). What to do after high school: The two-year versus four-year college enrollment decision. In R. G. Ehrenberg (Ed.), *Choices and consequences: Contemporary policy issues in education* (pp. 59–88). Ithaca, NY: ILR Press.

Rowan, H. (2006). *Predictors of delayed college enrollment and the impact of socioeconomic status.* Paper presented at annual meeting of the American Educational Research Association, San Francisco.

Rubin, L. (1976). *Worlds of pain: Life in the working class family.* New York: Basic Books.

St. John, E. P., Cabrera, A. F., Nora, A., and Asker, E. H. (2000). Economic influences on persistence reconsidered. How can finance research inform the reconceptualization of persistence models? In J. M. Braxton (Ed.), *Reworking the student departure puzzle* (pp. 29–47). Nashville, TN: Vanderbilt University Press.

St. John, E. P., Paulsen, M. B., and Carter, D. F. (2005). Diversity, college costs, and postsecondary opportunity: An examination of the financial nexus between college choice and persistence for African Americans and whites. *Journal of Higher Education, 76*(5), 545–569.

St. John, E. P., and Starkey, J. B. (1995). An alternative to net pricing: Assessing the influence of prices and subsidies on within year persistence. *Journal of Higher Education, 66*(2), 156–186.

Saunders, M., and Serna, I. (2004). Making college happen: The college experiences of first-generation Latino students. *Journal of Hispanic Higher Education, 3*(2), 146–163.

Schmidt, P. (2004, September 24). "Report card" spurs calls for change in academe: Ten-year analysis shows declines in affordability and access to college. *Chronicle of Higher Education,* pp. A1, A20–A21.

Segal, H. G., DeMeis, D. K., Wood, G. A., and Smith, H. L. (2001). Assessing future possible selves by gender and socioeconomic status using the anticipated life history measure. *Journal of Personality, 69*(1), 57–87.

Sennett, R., and Cobb, J. (1973). *Hidden injuries of class.* New York: Vintage Books.

Sewell, W. H., Haller, A. O., and Portes, A. (1994). The educational and early occupational attainment process. In D. B. Grusky (Ed.), *Social stratification: Class, race, and gender in sociological perspective* (pp. 410-420). Boulder, CO: Westview Press.

Sewell, W. H., and Hauser, R. M. (1975). *Education, occupation, and earnings: Achievement in the early career.* Orlando, FL: Academic Press.

Shattock, M. (1981). Demography and social class: The fluctuating demand for higher education in Britain. *European Journal of Education, 16*(3–4), 381–392.

Slaney, R. B., and Brown, M. T. (1983). Effects of race and socioeconomic status on career choice variables among collegiate men. *Journal of Vocational Behavior, 23,* 257–269.

Smart, J. C., and Pascarella, E. T. (1986). Socioeconomic achievements of former college students. *Journal of Higher Education, 57*(5), 529–549.

Solmon, L. (1975). The definition of college quality and its impact on earnings. *National Bureau of Economic Research, 2,* 537–587.

Solorzano, D. G., and Bernal, D. D. (2001). Examining transformational resistance through a critical race and LATCRIT theory framework: Chicana and Chicano students in an urban context. *Urban Education, 36*(3), 308–342.

Solorzano, D. G., and Villalpando, O. (1998). Critical race theory, marginality, and the experience of students of color in higher education. In C. A. Torres and T. R. Mitchell (Eds.), *Sociology of education: Emerging perspectives.* Albany: State University of New York Press.

Stitt-Gohdes, W. L. (1997). *Career development: Issues of gender, race, and class.* ERIC Clearinghouse on Adult, Career and Vocational Education Information Series, 371. ED 413533.

Suhr, J. (1980). *Study of the 1978 summer step: The summer "bridge" program at the learning skills center, University of California, Davis.* Davis: University of California, Office of Student Affairs Research and Evaluation. (Eric Document Reproduction Service No. ED256275)

Swail, W. S. (2000). Preparing America's disadvantaged for college: Programs that increase college opportunity. *New Directions for Institutional Research, 107,* 85–102.

Swail, W. S., Cabrera, A. F., and Lee, C. (2004). *Latino youth and the pathway to college.* Washington, DC: Educational Policy Institute.

Swail, W. S., and Perna, L. W. (2002). Pre-college outreach programs: A national perspective. In W. G. Tierney and L. S. Hagedorn (Eds.), *Increasing access to college* (pp. 15–34). Albany: State University of New York Press.

Tate IV, W. F. (1997). Critical race theory and education: History, theory, and implications. *Review of Research in Education, 22,* 195–247.

Tate IV, W. F. (2005). Ethics, engineering and the challenge of racial reform in education. *Race, Ethnicity and Education, 8*(1), 121–127.

Teranishi, R. T. (2002). Asian Pacific Americans and critical race theory: An examination of school racial climate. *Equity and Excellence in Education, 35*(2), 144–154.

Teranishi, R. T., Ceja, M., Antonio, A. L., Allen, W. R., and McDonough, P. M. (2004). The college choice process for Asian Pacific Americans: Ethnicity and socioeconomic class in context. *Review of Higher Education, 27*(4), 527–551.

Terenzini, P. T. Cabrera, A. F., and Bernal, E. M. (2001). *Swimming against the tide: The poor in American higher education.* Princeton, NJ: College Board.

Terenzini, P. T., Springer, L., Yaeger, P. M., Pascarella, E. T., and Nora, A. (1996). First-generation college students: Characteristics, experiences, and cognitive development. *Research in Higher Education, 26,* 161–179.

Tett, L. (2004). Mature working-class students in an "elite" university: Discourses of risk, choice, and exclusion. *Studies in the Education of Adults, 36*(2), 252–264.

Theodorson, G. A., and Theodorson, A. G. (1969). *A modern dictionary of sociology.* New York: HarperCollins.

Tierney, W. G., and Jun, A. (2001). A university helps prepare low income youths for college: Tracking student success. *Journal of Higher Education, 72*(2), 205–225.

Tinto, V. (1987). *Leaving college: Rethinking the causes and cures of student attrition.* Chicago: University of Chicago Press.

Tinto, V. (1993). *Leaving college: Rethinking the causes and cures of student attrition* (2nd ed.). Chicago: University of Chicago Press.

Tinto, V. (2006). Research and practice of student retention, What's next? *Journal of College Student Retention, 8*(1), 1–19.

Titus, M. A. (2006a). No college student left behind: The influence of financial aspects of a state's higher education policy on college completion. *Review of Higher Education, 29*(3), 293–317.

Titus, M. A. (2006b). *How social class influences college completion: An alternative examination of the role of parental wealth.* Paper presented at annual meeting of the American Educational Research Association, San Francisco.

Titus, M. A. (2006c). Understanding college degree completion of students with low socioeconomic status: The influence of the institutional financial context. *Research in Higher Education, 47*(4), 371–398.

Titus, M. A. (2006d). Understanding the influence of the financial context of institutions on student persistence at four-year colleges and universities. *Journal of Higher Education, 77*(2), 353–375.

Trusty, J., Robinson, C. R., Plata, M., and Ng, K. (2000). Effects of gender, socioeconomic status, and early academic performance on postsecondary educational choice. *Journal of Counseling and Development, 78,* 463–472.

U.S. Department of Education. National Center for Education Statistics. (2001). *Paving the way to postsecondary education: K-12 intervention programs for underrepresented youth* (NCES 2001–205). Washington, DC: National Center for Education Statistics.

U.S. Department of Education. Office of the Under Secretary, Policy and Program Studies Service. (2003). *National evaluation of GEAR UP, A summary of the first two years.* Rockville, MD: Westat.

U.S. Department of Education. Office of the Under Secretary. Policy and Program Studies Service. (2004). *The impacts of regular Upward Bound: Results from the third follow-up data collection.* Washington, DC: U.S. Department of Education.

U.S. Department of Education. (2006). *A test of leadership: Charting the future of U.S. higher education.* Washington, DC: U.S. Department of Education.

Useem, M. (1994). The inner circle. In D. B. Grusky (Ed.), *Social stratification: Class, race, and gender in sociological perspective* (pp. 223–232). Boulder, CO: Westview Press.

Useem, M., and Karabel, J. (1990). Pathways to top corporate management. In
P. W. Kingston and L. S. Lewis (Eds.), *The high status track: Studies of elite schools and
stratification*. Albany: State University of New York Press.

Valeri-Gold, M., Deming, M. P., and Stone, K. (1992). The bridge: A summer enrichment
program to retain African-American collegians. *Journal of the First-Year Experience and
Students in Transition, 4*(2), 101–117.

Wachtel, P. (1975). The effect of school quality on achievement, attainment levels, and lifetime earnings. *National Bureau of Economic Research, 2,* 502–536.

Walpole. M. (2003). Social mobility and college: Low SES students' experiences and outcomes of college. *Review of Higher Education, 27*(1), 45–73.

Walpole, M. (2004). *Socioeconomic status and college: Insights from Bourdieu and critical race
theory.* Paper presented at the annual meeting of the Association for the Study of Higher
Education, Kansas City, MO.

Walpole, M. (in press). Emerging from the pipeline: African American students nine years
after entering college. *Research in Higher Education.*

Walpole, M., McDonough, P. M., Bauer, C. J., Gibson, C., Kanyi, K. T., and Toliver, R.
(2005). This test is unfair: Urban African American and Latino high school students'
perceptions of standardized college admission tests. *Urban Education, 40*(3),
321–349.

Wassmer, R., Moore, C., and Shulock, N. (2004). Effect of racial/ethnic composition on
transfer rates in community colleges: Implications for policy and practice. *Research in
Higher Education, 45*(6), 651–672.

Weber, M. (1946). Class, status, party. In H. H. Gerth and C. W. Mills (Eds.), *From Max
Weber: Essays in sociology.* New York: Oxford University Press.

Wechsler, H. S. (1997). An academic Gresham's Law: Group repulsion as a theme in
American higher education. In L. F. Goodchild and H. S. Wechsler (Eds.), *The history of
higher education* (2nd ed., pp. 416–431). Boston: Pearson Custom Publishing.

Weis, L. (1992). Discordant voices in the urban community college. In L. S. Zwerling and
H. B. London (Eds.), *First generation students: Confronting the cultural issue* (pp. 13–27).
San Francisco: Jossey-Bass.

Where are the poor students? A conversation about social class and college attendance.
(2004, September-October). *About Campus,* 19–24.

Williams, M. L., Leppel, K., and Waldauer, C. (2005). Socioeconomic status and college major:
A reexamination of the empirical evidence. *Journal of the First Year Experience, 17*(2), 49–72.

Willis, P. (1977). *Learning to labor: How working class kids get working class jobs.* New York:
Columbia University Press.

Yosso, T. J. (2005). Whose culture has capital? A critical race theory discussion of community
cultural wealth. *Race, Ethnicity and Education, 8*(1), 69–91.

Youn, T.I.K., Arnold, K. D., and Salkever, K. (1999). *Pathways to prominence: The effects of
social origins and education on career achievements of American Rhodes scholars.* Paper
presented at the annual meeting of the Association for the Study of Higher Education,
San Antonio, TX.

Zweigenhaft, R. (1993). Prep school and public school graduates of Harvard: A longitudinal study of the accumulation of social and cultural capital. *Journal of Higher Education, 64,* 211–225.

Zweigenhaft, R. L., and Domhoff, G. W. (1991). *Blacks in the white establishment?* New Haven, CT: Yale University Press.

Name Index

A

Abbott, J., 36
Ackermann, S. P., 78, 81, 87
Adelman, C., 30, 37, 38, 39, 81, 86, 87
Ahlburg, D. A., 11
Akerhielm, K., 7, 9, 11, 12, 30, 31, 34, 37, 38, 39, 81, 86, 87
Allen, W. R., 66
Allmendinger, D., 1
Anderson, M. S., 29, 48, 53, 54, 57, 69, 71
Antonio, A. L., 22, 61, 62, 86
Archer, L., 13, 31, 36, 39
Armesto, M., 77, 78, 87
Arnold, K.D., 55
Arzy, M. R., 43, 45
Asker, E. H., 21
Astin, A. W., 1, 2, 7, 21, 29, 31, 41, 69, 70, 71, 73, 74, 81, 83, 87

B

Ball, S. J., 13, 36, 37, 64
Balz, F. J., 77, 78, 87
Bauer, C. J., 24
Beattie, I. R., 11, 17, 20, 27, 33, 61, 85
Becker, G. S., 17, 20
Bedsworth, W., 1, 2, 7, 15, 29, 34, 38, 39, 81
Berger, J. B., 7, 23
Bernal, E. M., 2, 17, 25, 26, 27
Bettinger, E. P., 77
Biklen, S., 83

Blake, J. H., 77
Blau, P. M., 9, 17, 18, 20
Boatsman, K. C., 51, 73
Bogdan, R., 83
Bohon, S. A., 64
Boli, J., 53, 54, 70, 74
Borrego, S. E., 29, 69, 75
Bourdieu, P., 3, 17, 21, 22, 23, 24, 26, 27, 67, 84
Bowen, W. G., 1, 2, 4, 15, 29, 30, 31, 69, 72, 74, 75
Bowles, S., 53, 54, 70, 71, 72, 84
Briggs, C., 61
Brown, M. T., 9, 10, 13, 56, 66
Buck, J., 78, 87
Burd, S., 77, 85
Burkhum, K. R., 2

C

Cabrera, A. F., 2, 7, 21, 30, 32, 38, 39, 48, 49, 57, 64, 81, 85, 86, 87
Cabrito, B. G., 13, 36
Carnevale, A. P., 7, 9, 11, 29, 31, 69, 70, 71, 73, 85
Carter, D. J., 17, 18, 19, 21, 27, 47, 62, 68, 71
Casey, J. G., 7, 9, 13, 44, 45
Castaneda, M. B., 21
Catsambis, S., 9, 75
Ceja, M., 63
Chen, X., 7, 35

Child, R. L., 77, 78
Choy, S. P., 7, 8, 9, 12, 30, 35, 38, 81
Chuateco, L. I., 10
Cicourel, A. V., 30
Clark, B., 70
Cobb, J., 30
Colby, S., 1
Coleman, J. S., 24
Conley, D., 19, 67
Connor, H., 13, 31, 36, 38, 39
Cookson, P. W., 3, 9, 31, 74, 75
Corcoran, M., 18, 19
Cuccaro-Alamin, S., 7, 8, 9, 12, 36, 38, 43, 45, 47, 50, 55, 70
Cureton, J. S., 83

D

Dale, S. B., 73
David, M., 13, 36
Davies, S., 11, 42
Davies, T. G., 43, 45
Davis, J. E., 59
DeMeis, D. K., 51
Deming, M. P., 78
Dennis, J. M., 10, 14, 44, 65
DesJardins, S. L., 11, 14, 34, 38, 39, 61, 85
Dixson, A. D., 25
Doctor, J., 1
Domhoff, G. W., 3, 31, 70, 71, 73, 74, 75
Doyle, S. K., 12, 44
DuBrock, C. P., 48
Duncan, O. D., 9, 17, 18, 20
Dynarski, S., 85

E

Egerton, M., 13, 36, 37, 38, 53, 55
Ekman, R., 76, 77
Esten, M. R., 77, 78, 87
Evans, R., 78

F

Farmer, H., 56
Fenske, R. H., 48, 57, 77, 85
Filkins, J. W., 12, 44

Fitts, J. D., 78
Fleming, J., 66
Francis, K., 78
Freeman, K., 30, 31, 59, 62, 81

G

Gandara, P., 38, 77, 87
Garcia, P., 78, 87
Garth, R., 76, 77
Gaskell, J., 30
Geranios, 77
Gibbons, M. M., 35, 38, 56
Gibson, C., 24
Gilbert, D., 3
Gintis, H., 53, 54, 70, 71, 72, 84
Gladieux, L. E., 1, 48, 81, 85
Goldrick-Rab, S., 32, 38
Goldstein, M. S., 7, 9, 13, 45, 51, 53, 55, 72, 73
Gorman, B. K., 64
Goyette, K. A., 9, 10, 12, 41, 42, 45, 53, 54, 56, 57, 82
Guppy, N., 11, 42, 45

H

Hacker, A., 3
Hagedorn, L. S., 70
Halle, D., 30
Haller, A. O., 9
Halsey, A. H., 13, 36, 38
Hamrick, F. A., 24, 33, 60, 87
Han, S. W., 32, 38
Haniff, N. Z., 66
Harbour, C. P., 43
Harker, R. K., 23
Hauser, R. M., 9, 17, 18, 19, 20
Hearn, J. C., 1, 2, 7, 29, 31, 48, 53, 54, 57, 69, 71, 74, 81
Heller, D. E., 20, 75, 85
Hoffnung, R. J., 51, 71, 72, 73
Hooker, M., 7
Horn, L., 7, 35, 47, 49, 57
Horvat, E. M., 17, 22, 23, 24, 30, 62, 81
Hossler, D., 2, 32, 35
Hurtado, S., 61, 62

Trent, J., 22
Trusty, J., 43, 45
Turner, E., 13
Tyree, A., 9

U

Useem, M., 47, 55, 70, 71, 73, 74

V

Valeri-Gold, M., 78, 87
Vantresca, M., 17, 23
Venezia, A., 86
Vesper, N., 2, 35
Villalpando, O., 17, 25, 26, 27

W

Wachtel, P., 53
Waldauer, C., 7, 9
Walpole, M., 7, 9, 10, 17, 22, 23, 24, 27,
    30, 38, 39, 41, 42, 43, 45, 47, 48, 51,
    52, 53, 56, 59, 64, 68, 81, 82, 83, 84, 87

Wassmer, R., 70
Weber, M., 8, 9, 18, 24
Wechsler, H. S., 1
Weininger, E. B., 24
Weis, L., 67
Williams, M. L., 7, 9, 10, 42, 45
Willis, P., 23, 30, 31
Wise, D. A., 7, 35
Wishengrad, R., 78
Wolniak, G. C., 7
Wood, G. A., 51

Y

Yaeger, P. M., 7, 44
Yosso, T. J., 17, 24, 25
Youn, T.I.K., 55, 71, 74

Z

Zweigenhaft, R., 31, 53, 54, 70, 73,
    74, 75

Subject Index

A

African American
    college choice, 60, 61–63
    experiences and outcomes, 64–65
American dream, myth of, 3
Asian American
    college choice, 63
    experiences and outcomes, 65, 66
Aspirations, educational, 47, 51–52
Assistance, programmatic, 75–79

B

Bourdieu's framework, 17, 21–24, 27
Bridge programs, 77–79
Britain
    college choice in, 64
    social class and college enrollment in, 36

C

Career orientation, 56
College access
    conclusions on, 37–39
    parental education and, 35–36
    parental income and, 34–35
    parental occupation and, 36–37
    prior educational experiences and, 30–31
    socioeconomic status and, 31–33
College choice process, 60–64
College experiences
    conclusions on, 45
    parental education and, 43–44
    parental income and, 43

    parental occupation and, 44–45
    socioeconomic status and, 41–43
College outcomes
    aspirations and, 47, 51–52
    career orientation and, 56
    conclusions on, 56–57
    graduate school attendance, income, and occupational status, 53–56
    learning outcomes and, 52
    persistence and, 48–51
College-going rates of low-SES students, 1–2
Community colleges
    student attainment at, 71
    transfer rates at, 70
Cost of college and subsequent earnings, 73
Critical race theory, 17, 24–26

D

Definitions
    complexity of, 7–8
    disunity of, 13–14
    historical development of categories, 8–10
    of EEC students, 14–16
    of parental education, 12
    of parental income, 11–12
    of parental occupation, 13
    of socioeconomic status, 10–11

E

Economically and educationally challenged (EEC) students

About the Author

MaryBeth Walpole is an associate professor in the Educational Leadership Department at Rowan University. She earned her Ph.D. in higher education and organizational change from UCLA. Her research interests focus on access and equity issues within the college arena, including the effects of social class and racial background on college admission, attendance, experiences, and outcomes; and how the type of institutions attended shape students' experiences and outcomes.

About the ASHE Higher Education Report Series

Since 1983, the ASHE (formerly ASHE-ERIC) Higher Education Report Series has been providing researchers, scholars, and practitioners with timely and substantive information on the critical issues facing higher education. Each monograph presents a definitive analysis of a higher education problem or issue, based on a thorough synthesis of significant literature and institutional experiences. Topics range from planning to diversity and multiculturalism, to performance indicators, to curricular innovations. The mission of the Series is to link the best of higher education research and practice to inform decision making and policy. The reports connect conventional wisdom with research and are designed to help busy individuals keep up with the higher education literature. Authors are scholars and practitioners in the academic community. Each report includes an executive summary, review of the pertinent literature, descriptions of effective educational practices, and a summary of key issues to keep in mind to improve educational policies and practice.

The Series is one of the most peer reviewed in higher education. A National Advisory Board made up of ASHE members reviews proposals. A National Review Board of ASHE scholars and practitioners reviews completed manuscripts. Six monographs are published each year and they are approximately 120 pages in length. The reports are widely disseminated through Jossey-Bass and John Wiley & Sons, and they are available online to subscribing institutions through Wiley InterScience (http://www.interscience.wiley.com).

Call for Proposals

The ASHE Higher Education Report Series is actively looking for proposals. We encourage you to contact one of the editors, Dr. Kelly Ward (kaward@wsu.edu) or Dr. Lisa Wolf-Wendel (lwolf@ku.edu), with your ideas.

Recent Titles